BEYOND THE SHALLOWS

Life Is Better in the Deep End

BEYOND THE SHALLOWS

JASON HUNDLEY

LEAFWOOD
PUBLISHERS
an imprint of Abilene Christian University Press

BEYOND THE SHALLOWS

Life Is Better in the Deep End

LEAFWOOD PUBLISHERS
an imprint of Abilene Christian University Press

ISBN 978-1-68426-093-5 | LCCN 2024033310

Printed in the United States of America

Published in association with The Blythe Daniel Agency, Inc., PO Box 64197, Colorado Springs, CO 80962.

LIBRARY OF CONGRESS CATALOGING-IN-PUBLICATION DATA
Names: Hundley, Jason, author.
Title: Beyond the shallows : life is better in the deep end / Jason Hundley.
Description: Abilene, Texas : Leafwood Publishers, 2025. | Includes bibliographical references.
Identifiers: LCCN 2024033309 (print) | LCCN 2024033310 (ebook) | ISBN 9781684260935 | ISBN 9781684268467 (ebook)
Subjects: LCSH: Self-actualization (Psychology)—Religious aspects—Christianity. | Self-realization—Religious aspects—Christianity. | Christian life.
Classification: LCC BV4598.2 .H84 2025 (print) | LCC BV4598.2 (ebook) | DDC 248.4—dc23/eng/20241120
LC record available at https://lccn.loc.gov/2024033309
LC ebook record available at https://lccn.loc.gov/2024033310

Cover design by Greg Jackson, Thinkpen Design | Interior text design by Sandy Armstrong, Strong Design

Leafwood Publishers is an imprint of Abilene Christian University Press
ACU Box 29138 | Abilene, Texas 79699

1-877-816-4455 | www.leafwoodpublishers.com

25 26 27 28 29 30 31 / 7 6 5 4 3 2 1

To Emily, who has the most beautiful heart
I have ever encountered.

CONTENTS

AUTHOR'S NOTE

This is the book I wish I had in my hands as I walked onto my college campus. As you will find in my story, the church that raised me taught me much more about the heart than the average pew dweller. While by no means perfect, it changed the trajectory of my life for the better. I pray that this book will give you the tools you need to see the instructions in Scripture in a new light. I hope you would not see a list of things to do or not to do, but that every command would be seen in light of God's love for you. You will see how merciful he is in giving us structure and the best way to live our lives here on planet Earth.

I found as I wrote, I had to hold back from quoting too many verses to prove that my opinions were true. I have actively avoided this strategy when writing this book. Instead, I have written my thoughts and a key verse that links the thought to the theme of the heart in Scripture. This made the writing process far more enjoyable for me, and I hope the reading process is also enjoyable for you. However, be aware that my goal is not to defend a position but to unpack a major theme in God's Word.

To help you get the most out of this book, I have divided it into three parts. The first section of the book is designed to give you an idea of how much better life would be if you knew what was going on in your heart. The Bible is very concerned with the status of your heart, and that should be a clue that it is an important piece of the puzzle when it comes to living a full and abundant life. This section also shows you the ways that sin and the enemy have targeted your heart. This journey, like most things, is worth the effort but also takes a lot of work.

Section Two of the book is where I will give you a framework for your heart. This is where you will learn all about the levels beneath the surface of your heart and how to access them. While it is very simple in nature, the act of exploring your heart is challenging and rewarding. As you learn to master your heart, become vulnerable, and build community, serving others' hearts becomes a high priority. Section Three addresses how to approach these skills biblically and with discernment.

Much like the good stuff lies beneath the surface of your heart, the deeper you dig into Scripture, the richer the treasure you will find. Once your curiosity about the heart is piqued, apply that same curiosity to your Bible study. Get curious about the motives and methods that Jesus uses to touch the hearts of those around him. Allow yourself to wonder at the way he is able to impact your heart thousands of years after he spoke the words of life recorded in Scripture. Stay curious, keep asking why, and find the theme of the heart. It will always be linked directly or indirectly to Jesus. Find him in the Bible, and keep him in the very center of your heart.

Jason Hundley

ACKNOWLEDGMENTS

I began my journey as an author by accident. Sick in bed during the early stages of the pandemic, I was quarantined from my own family and ran out of things I wanted to watch on TV. I picked up my computer and started writing. Many weeks later when I felt that my manuscript was complete, I contacted Blythe Daniel, who is now my literary agent. She graciously took the time to tell me what I needed to do in order to pitch my book to her. I now know that I did everything either wrong or in the wrong order from the standard industry procedures. Blythe simply told me over the phone, "You just started writing, and there is nothing wrong with that." I owe a tremendous amount of thanks to the Blythe Daniel Agency. You have set me on the right path and championed me so well.

I also want to thank ACU Press and Leafwood Publishing. I am thrilled to be working with people who understand the role that the heart plays in the lives of young people. Thank you to Jason Fikes for helping me finish my manuscript and for your guidance. I also want to thank my editor and copyeditor, Mary Hardegree and Marissa Earl. I love collaborative work, and the book is better because of your involvement.

Berean Bible Church in Knoxville, Tennessee, and Fellowship Bible Church in Dalton, Georgia, are major parts of this book. Thank you to Pastor John Stone, who is home with Jesus, and the entire Stone family. I hope that his legacy lives on through the lessons I learned directly or indirectly because of his ministry to me. Tab Jordan, who still comments "warrior" on my teaching content online, your influence on my life is ongoing and powerful. Thank you for investing in me when I needed it most. Fred Freed, there is little I could write that would accurately sum up the impact your example and training on this topic have meant to me over the years. Thank you for believing in me and equipping me for all these years. Tim Chaney, thank you for being my sounding board and helping me figure out how to get this giant plane of an idea off the runway. Barbara Challies, thank you for your insights and guidance. Thank you, Jim and Dr. Helen McIntosh, for your unwavering belief in me. Thank you to my parents, Chris and Donna Hundley, who were my spiritual sherpas and so patient with me while I found my heart in Christ. Thank you to my sister, Jessi, who walked much of this journey of discovering the heart with me. Thank you to the many people in these two communities and many other family and friends who have supported me and my family and made this book a reality.

Finally, thank you to my kids, Wyatt, Logan, Ellie, and Mia, who had to put up with me sitting behind a keyboard, and to Emily, my wife. It has been a joy to see you discover these truths alongside me during our marriage. Thank you for believing in me, even when I want to leave comfortable circumstances to pursue the extraordinary. You are my greatest treasure and most wonderful adventure.

SECTION ONE

CHAPTER ONE

WHAT'S WRONG WITH THE FOUNTAIN?

Have you ever seen a fountain after someone pours in an entire bottle of Dawn dish soap? I have, and let me tell you, it's a thing of beauty. Now, this is by no means a confession of guilt from the author, but if you have not had the pleasure of witnessing something like this, let me fill you in. The process begins without fanfare. Within minutes, there are a few bubbles in the bottom of the fountain, but no more than your average toddler's bathtub experience. It isn't until minute four that things begin to pick up.

The original thought behind bubbles in a fountain is specifically that: bubbles *in* a fountain. Bubbles, however, are not concerned about the limitations we would like to put on them. They just keep coming. Eventually, the fountain will bubble up so high that you begin to worry it will soon take over the whole courtyard. It is at this point that you start thinking, "This was not my best idea."

We all make mistakes. Some mistakes are manageable. In fact, many mistakes you make have little to no effect on your life as a whole, like stubbing your toe and using some language that doesn't make your mom proud. A small percentage of the mistakes you make can be helpful when you learn from them. This is called failing forward, and I am a big fan of progress through trial and error.

There is a different category of mistakes, however, that we want to avoid altogether. These mistakes have roots. These mistakes are drawing from something sinister and dark within us and leave no room for self-improvement, such as the personal attack we aimed at a loved one in the midst of a fight. We might not even believe what we said because the goal was to hurt the other person. It wasn't premeditated, but it did create the desired effect in the moment. This category of mistakes is like Dawn dish soap in a public fountain. They start insignificantly, quickly grow into a real problem, and then we are left to hope that their effects will dissipate with time. If only all our mistakes were so easily dissolved as bubbles in a fountain.

We know the pain of a mistake that lingers. If we are honest, we have a truckload of mistakes to carry. None of us is unique in this regard; we all have mistakes that follow us through life. Some people call it baggage, some people call it sin, and some people call it trauma. No matter what label we want to slap on it, the truth is that it is weighing us down, destroying our relationships, and controlling us. The problem with sin is that it doesn't just stay contained within us. We alone don't feel the consequences of our sin. There is always collateral damage. This can range from relatively insignificant damage to life-ending damage. What we choose to overlook about the nature of our sin is this: Sin ignored has more opportunity to destroy our lives.

THE BIBLICAL HEART

This is why Jesus and the Bible have so much to say about your heart. Now, I am not talking about the organ that keeps blood pumping through your veins, but rather your spiritual heart. The part of you that is life-giving to who you are. You may call it your "inner being" or "the voice inside your head." In the Bible, the heart involves everything that comes together to make you you. Your will, your desires, your dreams, your passions, your personality, your motivations, your inner being, the thing that gives you your "you-ness." It is your emotional, spiritual, and mental all wrapped up into one word: heart. There is no escaping your heart. There is no trading for someone else's heart. You can, however, install some upgrades to your heart.

The heart is mentioned roughly one thousand times in Scripture. Clearly, God is concerned with our hearts, so we should be as well. God has the best information available to us about how to live life abundantly, so the things that are important to him should be important to us. He has intentionally placed each atom, neuron, and cell in our bodies and made them home to our souls. You are unlike anything that has ever been or will be in the future, and God cares deeply that you steward your unique heart in this short life on Earth.

The big picture that Scripture paints about our hearts is that the status of our hearts is deeply connected to the status of our relationship with God. Remember that our hearts are made up of our emotional, mental, and spiritual health. That means all those separate elements of emotion, mental stability, and spiritual well-being move in harmony with each other. If we grow in one, we grow in all areas. They work together in tandem. Not only that, but everything we say, think, or do comes directly from our hearts and into the world. There are limitless possibilities for positive and negative things to come out of our hearts and spill into our lives. Just like a fountain. That is why the wisest man in history admonished his son to "keep your heart with all vigilance, for from it flow the springs of life" (Prov. 4:23).

King Solomon was that wise man, and he knew that the heart acts like a fountain. Just like our Dawn dish soap fountain overflowed with bubbles, our hearts are uncontrollably overflowing with "the springs of life." The problem is our lack of control over what is coming out of our hearts. I know it's not what we want to admit to ourselves, but without understanding and regular attention given to our hearts, we have no control over what is spilling out of them and into our lives. That is why understanding and applying this verse is central to this book.

So, what does it mean to "keep your heart with all vigilance"? Reading multiple translations of this verse is helpful when trying to understand Solomon's full message. The NIV says, "Above all else, guard your heart, for everything you do flows from it" (Prov. 4:23). So which is it? Are we supposed to guard our hearts or keep our hearts? The word "guard" in this context is challenging. I understand the reason why the translators would use this word. If we are guarding something, it implies that what we are guarding is valuable. Certainly, if the Bible mentions the heart so frequently, it is valuable to God and should also be valuable to us.

We know inherently that our hearts are valuable. Unfortunately, knowing a heart is valuable is not enough to get us to act appropriately. Just ask any teenager who has gone through a breakup if they feel like their heart was valued. All of us carry regrets from past relationships. These hurt for so long because of the damage they do to the heart. Breakups show us where we have undervalued our own hearts, or worse, where another person did not respect the value of our hearts. So often it is only pain that causes us to start valuing our hearts, but the verse does not stop there. Not only are our hearts valuable, but we are to guard them because they are fragile.

THE FRAGILE HEART

Remember, the biblical, spiritual heart is not just feelings and emotions but our desires and will as well. As a pastor, I have seen people get old. Nothing shows us the depths of our hearts' fragility like age. The good news is that sometimes people age slowly. I know a gentleman who was told at fifty that he would start to see a physical and mental decline. It didn't happen. Five years passed, and he still felt spry. Five more years, same story. Finally, a few weeks after his seventieth birthday, he told me that it felt like he hit an invisible wall. The effects of time, though delayed, finally caught up to him. This conversation was the first time in seven years of knowing him that I would have described him as fragile.

Unfortunately, this is not the same story for many who have aged in my church. Some have strokes. One day, they are functional and lively; the next day, they are trapped within their own minds. They are fully aware but unable to move or speak like they used to. Ask anyone who has lived through that experience, and they will tell you the human heart is fragile. A profound tenderness and value are placed on each moment of life when people learn to exist in this state. Suddenly, all the big plans and schemes these dear saints spent a lifetime building evaporate. They are left making the most out of life with limited mobility. If we are wise and interact with people in this stage of life, we begin to care more about the status of our hearts because we understand how fragile they are.

Solomon's challenge for us is not to guard our hearts as if to imprison them but rather to take good care of them, like a plant that needs regular attention to flourish. The goal is not self-preservation and the avoidance of pain but to be aware of our hearts' needs, pains, hopes, and dreams. We can think of the heart like a raised-bed garden. If left untended, even though it is separated from the rest of the lawn, it will be overrun with weeds and plants that yield no harvest. To see the vegetation we have planted yield a worthwhile crop, we must tend to the garden.

Our hearts are the same. If we want to see fruit from our Bible study, if we want to have the sermon stick with us throughout the week, if we want our prayer life to increase, and if we want to get something of value from worship, we must also tend to our hearts. Ultimately, our goal as believers is to become more like Jesus. We should remember that Jesus was always telling parables and stories because this strategy of teaching circumvents the brain and speaks to the heart. Jesus was perfect in his ability to identify and speak to the heart. To become more like him, we should want to do the same.

THE WORK

Our hearts require regular maintenance. That is what this verse means by "with all vigilance." The journey to understanding and addressing the issues of the heart is neither easy nor fast. Rather, this skill requires a tremendous amount of work that gets easier only with experience. It is tempting to look at a challenge, such as the foggy mess that is our heart, and think, "Man, I hope I only have to do this once." Things that take vigilance are never one-and-done. I hate taking out the trash, mowing the lawn, or cleaning the toilets, but that is part of being a homeowner. It doesn't matter how well I am able to clean a toilet or maintain my lawn one week if I don't do it faithfully the next week and the week after that. In the same way, King Solomon knew that our hearts require regular attention in order to stay healthy. That is why we can have an incredible breakthrough in counseling—with our self-image, in our attitude toward work—and then backtrack within a matter of weeks. We must apply vigilance to our hearts in order to yield lasting benefits.

There will be seasons in our lives when our hearts require a lot of our time and effort. These challenging seasons are often when God does a lot of work in our lives over a short period of time. However, regular maintenance of our hearts can make the breakthroughs more frequent, less painful, and more fruitful. The challenge is to stay vigilant.

WHEN WE DON'T STICK WITH IT

There is a massive shift happening in the church. According to *The Great Dechurching*, there are more people leaving the church now than during the first and second great awakenings and every other revival combined.[1] The book dives deep into the numbers to try to explain why this is happening, what demographics are affected, and what we can do to direct people back to God and his church.

The biggest shock to me was that the main reason people give when asked why they left the church is because they moved. This is less a reason and more a thinly veiled excuse. I understand that moving is challenging and finding a new community of like-minded believers takes time and effort, but it is clear to me that most people just wanted an easy out. Clearly, there is something wrong on a heart level.

I would like to believe that most people who were regularly attending before leaving their church were there because of some significant spiritual growth. If that is the case, what happened? We have an epidemic of unguarded hearts. Something that at one time propelled people to life change and spiritual growth has not sustained them for a lifetime of investing in

God's church. I would go so far as to venture that, in most cases, people moved for good reasons. It was never their intention to distance themselves from the church, but even good things can steal our focus and slowly lead us astray from what we really want in life.

It is tricky to guard the heart. It is not always self-destructive habits or rage inside our hearts that impede our spiritual growth. More often, the seemingly good things that we elevate or inflate to an unhealthy degree chip away at our hearts, drawing our affections away from a deeper relationship with God. That is why it is imperative that we stay vigilant with our hearts.

FAULTY FOUNTAINS

Our hearts are fountains full of Dawn dish soap. We can guard them, keep them, and tend to them with vigilance, but the one thing we can't do is stop them. The things that are on the inside are going to come out. The good and the bad will come to the surface. It doesn't matter how we attempt to hide it. Hiding our hearts is never an option. At some point, the pressure will be released, and the mess we end up with will be far worse than if we had dealt with the problem in the first place.

This book is not going to teach you how to put a spiritual cork in your heart and try to make yourself look the part of the perfect Christian. Quite the opposite. According to the verse we are studying in this chapter, stopping the flow out of our hearts is not an option. That has not kept us from trying to stop up our hearts.

Stopping up our hearts is commonly referred to as bottling up our emotions, but it is so much more than that. It is far more dangerous as well. People can only take so much before they snap. If you have ever been around when someone who seems to be in control loses control, it is simultaneously terrifying and pathetic. While everyone's fuse is a different length, it seems to be the ones who bottle up their thoughts, dreams, passions, motives, and sins that explode to cause the most long-term damage to those around them.

I am incredibly thankful for the cultural push toward counseling. I feel that social acceptance for seeking counseling was becoming commonplace even before the world was thrown into a pandemic and the need became desperate. While one-on-one counseling is helpful and good, it alone will not fix the problems we have with our fountain hearts. It can help us identify some key points of damage to the fountain; it may even reveal some of the underlying problems, but we will always be responsible for what is coming out. Just like Dawn dish soap entered the inner workings of the fountain, sin has contaminated the contents of the fountains of our hearts and spilled out onto the people in our lives. It doesn't matter how much we try to hide it; the effects of sin are out of control. They start small and spread without concern for the boundaries we would place on them.

There is hope if you are looking for a way to find freedom from habitual sin. There is healing if you are injured by abuse and can't seem to find life after living through such heinous experiences. There is a better future for you if you can't seem to be in control of your anger, jealousy, fear, depression, anxiety, or feelings of worthlessness. Your heart may be flowing ungoverned, spilling over your life and those close to you with disastrous effects, but there is hope.

REPAIR OR REPLACE?

God doesn't just want to fix our hearts; he wants to give us new hearts. It is like a contractor looking at a condemned house. He could try to salvage all the framing and timber and repair all the damaged places, but at a certain point, it is more cost-effective to tear down the structure, shore up the foundation, and start again.

The only way we can win at what matters most in this life is with a new heart from God. That is the only way we can build a foundation that lasts and endures the storms that come. However, a new heart is like a new vehicle. In a new car, it takes practice to work all the knobs and levers effortlessly. In the same way, a new spiritual heart from God has the same function as our old heart but takes practice to use to its fullest.

There is one practical change we can make today to help get the most out of the new spiritual heart God has to offer. Humble our hearts. First John says it this way: "If we confess our sins to him, he is faithful and just to forgive us our sins and to cleanse us from all wickedness" (1 John 1:9 NLT).

This verse is not just for the lost but also for believers. There is ample forgiveness and grace available to you and to me. That is the wonderful thing about forgiveness: You either have it or you do not. Once you have it, there is no need to question if you still have access to it. Jesus simply asks us to admit that we need it. We can find deep wells of joy in being cleansed from all in our hearts that doesn't look like Jesus. Once you experience his grace, trust me, you'll keep coming back for more, as I have. He has plenty to spare.

The heart posture of humility is incredibly important. The new heart is a gift from heaven. We learn how to use it in three places: in relationship with God, in the Bible, and in relationships with other believers. God desperately wants to reveal to us the secrets of our new heart, but he wants us to admit our need: "Come close to God, and God will come close to you. Wash your hands, you sinners; purify your hearts, for your loyalty is divided between God and the world" (James 4:8 NLT).

We can also humble our hearts by submitting to Scripture. The Bible is God's Word. It is how he has revealed himself to us, and it is how he wants to speak to us. He has the best knowledge about who we are and how we operate and has shared that in the Bible. The more we humble ourselves and listen to what it says, the more we will learn how to operate our new hearts. If you want to see a good example of this in action, I encourage you to read Psalm 139.

The third way to humble our hearts is to pursue healthy relationships where we can be vulnerable. This practice of finding deep friendships or mentors is so overlooked that I have included an entire chapter on this topic. For now, I will just say that God has used spiritually rich relationships in my life to speak clearly to me. I bet you have often prayed, "God, if I could just hear you speak, that would confirm everything." We all long for God to speak directly to us, but sometimes we don't hear it. He is not silent; when we need it most, God can use people to hear us, hug us, hold us up, and encourage us. If we humble ourselves before some people who are close to God, we will find lifelong friendship. These relationships can help us continually grow in our faith.

WHERE THE WATER COMES FROM

Jesus said that he is the way, the truth, and the life (John 14:6). The springs of life in Proverbs 4:23 is a direct reference to a river that flows at the base of the Tree of Life. This tree is a fascinating study, but all we need to know for now is that Jesus is the way to access the pure, eternal waters that bring life. He alone can give us pure water for the fountain of our hearts. I hope you have the honor to meet someone familiar with these waters. There are precious few souls I have met that go beyond simply living out of the reality of a new heart in Christ and understand what it means to touch eternity with their hearts. My former pastor, John Stone, was one. He is no longer living, but I can still hear him picking out shockingly high harmony parts to old hymns as he walked our church halls.

It was during an internship at my church that I began to realize the true depth of spiritual fulfillment that Jesus has to offer. Every Thursday, I was involved in a three-hour prayer meeting with Pastor Stone and a handful of other pastoral staff and elders. If three hours sounds like a long time to be praying, it's because it is. Especially for someone in their late teens. The first time I attended a meeting, I simply kept changing between sitting and kneeling to try to keep myself awake. After a while, I noticed a pattern in the prayer. While I would chime in occasionally with a prayer request, Pastor Stone would follow my prayer by praising God for one of his attributes. Finally, he told me that for the first hour or so of the prayer meeting, the rest of the guys focus their attention not on their needs but exclusively on praising God. Suddenly, prayer meetings were not boring. Up until that time, I had never challenged myself to pray, sing, or even think about ways to praise God without the promise of getting anything in return. I love a challenge. It became a personal goal of mine to see how long I could go in prayer before I mentioned myself at all.

Pastor Stone's passion for deepening his relationship with God was beginning to infect me. I began to understand what made him a great teacher, counselor, and pastor. He was not afraid to spend a significant amount of time exclusively in the pursuit of praising God and his relationship with Jesus. Is that not the most common explanation of what heaven will be? Doesn't heaven involve an eternity of praising God and getting close to Jesus that never gets old or boring? That is what it means to access the eternal, living water our hearts desperately need. I won't promise that you will never get bored at a prayer meeting again, but accessing this stream is accessing life. My pastor knew that. He directed his heart's attention to God, not on itself. In return, God filled his heart with water from the river of life.

JESUS AND THE HEART

The more we discover who Jesus is, the more we will come to realize that his focus is always on the heart. When he corrects the Pharisees, he addresses their hearts, not their arguments. When he talks to his disciples, he trains them by speaking to the motivations of their hearts. When he hung on the cross in our place, even then, he asked the Father to forgive his murderers because they didn't "know what they [were] doing" (Luke 23:34 NLT). He knew they were blind to the motivations of their hearts.

Not you. You will not be blind to the things of your heart. You will press in to know yourself, past the depths of your sin and the pains of this life, and find a rich, fulfilling, and deep life. Humble yourself at the foot of the cross and find freedom, abundant life, and the security that comes with knowing who you are in Christ. That is how you win at what matters most—living from the inside out.

The only way to fix the fountain is by replacing the fountain and fixing the source of the water. So many of us have continued to pour dish soap into the fountain and then wonder why our spiritual lives feel stuck. Jesus offers freedom from a stuck life. He simply needs our hearts. Sin is not one-dimensional. There are layers upon layers. He will peel them back, expose them, and offer us something much better. He offers us a life that wins at what matters most.

God the Father, the Son, and the Holy Spirit, help me to know my heart. I know that my heart has been pouring out a lot of things that do not honor you. I need a remedy. I need a complete heart transplant. I want you to restore my heart, to be the foundation of my life, and to be the reason that I win at what matters most. I believe you want more good things for my life. I want to touch something eternal and to lead others to do the same. Help me to be everything that you created me to be and help me live out of the reality of having a new heart.

Amen

NOTE

[1] Jim Davis and Michael Graham, with Ryan P. Burge, *The Great Dechurching: Who's Leaving, Why Are They Going, and What Will It Take to Bring Them Back* (Zondervan, 2023).

CHAPTER TWO

A HEART WELL-FED

The sun beat down on me as I stood on the small floating dock on Haig Mill Lake. There, fishing is less about catching and releasing water-dwelling animals and more about catching some sunshine and releasing anxiety. My sons and I had loaded up three poles and a small tackle box so we could travel light. On the short but beautiful walk through the woods, we encountered a squirrel that showed no fear of people. We may not have caught any fish, but I would wager that we could have caught that squirrel if we wanted.

We know that when the weather turns warm and the radiant saucer magnolia in our yard decides to put on a show with its large purple-and-white leaves, the fish at the lake will be biting soon. The time has come for allergy medication and sunscreen to become a part of everyday life yet again. In the back of my mind, a subtle and persistent thought rests itself on my subconscious. It says, "I wonder when I can go to the lake again?"

However, mowing the lawn, spring-cleaning the house, and putting our winter clothes into storage are not the types of things that end up on the calendar. Don't misunderstand; I have no problem doing responsible adult things like mowing, cleaning, and storing stuff, but when I have spent a week dreaming of hungry fish and a pristine lake, I don't want to do responsible adult things. I know that we need to do the responsible thing, but I want to go fishing. I don't tell anyone I want to do that, because it would feel irresponsible to admit that I would shirk my responsibilities to do the fun thing. Rather, what I want is for my wife to read my mind, understand what time of year it is, and suggest that I take my kids to some body of water to fish.

I am sure that this is a major shock to you, but my wife doesn't read my mind. So when we discuss the plan for the day, there is no mention of fishing, and I begin to sulk. I put on a bad attitude like a pair of polarized sunglasses and do the "right thing" with slouched shoulders and a melancholy look on my face. All because my uncommunicated expectation went unmet. This feels silly to say, but this happens all the time. Failing to be honest with myself and my wife about what I would like turns me into a selfish grump.

TO BE KNOWN AND LOVED

Each of us has a universal desire to be known. The surge in the diversity of personality quizzes and resources is indicative of a generation that wants to know how they work and who they are. I am no exception to this trend. In high school, it was the DiSC profile. The four letters represent personality traits that could help you identify how you process the world and your relationships. It was helpful to see how dominant and direct my personality was, and I started working on softening some of my hard edges.

In college, there was a faction of my friends who dove into the Myers-Briggs personality test. INTJ, INFP, ESFJ, ENTP, and every other combination of confusing letters flooded my friends' conversations about how we are to interact with and understand each other. I never could remember all the different combinations, so it was only marginally helpful to me at the time.

My favorite test was the Enneagram. For some reason, this test made more sense than many of the others. I dove into understanding the motivations of each number, especially my own and my wife's numbers. It gave me some freedom to operate out of my passions and recognize harmful patterns in my attitudes and actions. It even gave me permission to pursue things that aligned with my passions that, for some reason, I hadn't pursued before.

For this reason, I love personality tests. They can help us tremendously when we are trying to understand the unique ways God has created us. They are particularly helpful when we need a framework for how other people think. However, they can also be harmful. The problem is the purpose of the tests. While the creators of these tools would have us understand ourselves better, we may find that we are tempted to take it a step further and see the tests as permission for unhealthy behavior.

For example, when I discovered that I was an Enneagram Three, the Achiever, it made me feel like I had permission to become a workaholic. If "high achiever" is who God made me to be, then why not do everything in my power to achieve regardless of the consequences? It took a lot of self-control and conversations with my wife to help me realign myself with what could be done in a realistic timeframe.

The problem is not the test; it's not my Enneagram number. The problem is that I lost sight of something far more important than my personality classification. I lost sight of Jesus. I climbed off the altar of surrender. I stopped wanting to become like him and decided that being me was enough. Now, this is tricky because God has absolutely designed us with particular gifts and talents to operate within. Still, those special gifts in no way remove our responsibility to become more like Jesus.

What would Jesus's personality test reveal? If he were to take the Myers-Briggs, Enneagram, or DiSC profile test, what do you think the test would show? I am not sure I know the answer to that question. However, I do know that if I give way to the flaws I see in my own personality type, I become less like Jesus in a hurry. While the goal is not perfection, becoming more like Christ is an integral part of growing up as a member of God's family. Somehow you and I are called to Christlikeness while still maintaining our individuality. Therefore, if we want to be more like Jesus, we cannot use our calling, passions, personality, or predispositions as a crutch or an excuse to ignore our calling to become more like him.

How important is it to you to become more like Jesus? Can you identify anything in your life that is in opposition to that goal or that is pulling you more away from him? I know that no matter how much love I feel for him in one moment, I am prone to drift from my affections. I'm doing the best I can, but it's hard at times. We face both internal and external opposition when we choose to follow Christ over what seems right to us. There are obstacles to our spiritual growth that remain on the landscape of our hearts. Sometimes, these idols aren't seen by others, but we know they are inside us. For me, one of the innocent-looking obstacles to maturing in my relationship with Christ is unmet expectations.

A personality test does not help me with the problem of unmet expectations (like my fishing example). Certainly, it may identify a problem like why I would resist open communication of my expectations, but it does nothing to address the selfish nature underneath the actions I take. Philippians 2:3 (NLT) says: "Don't be selfish; don't try to impress others. Be humble, thinking of others as better than yourselves." Is it wrong to want to fish? No. It is the motivation flowing from within my heart that is out of place. I can see in my life that when I value what I want more than what someone else needs, I am out of line. Helping someone else's heart often involves sacrificing my own.

This is why matters of the heart are so much more powerful to give us life change than personality tests or self-help resources. Don't misunderstand me. I love books that get my mind right. I am never more productive than when I have just read some incredible wisdom dropped from some of my favorite authors. I love to accomplish tasks and complete goals more than anyone I know. There is a temptation to assume that this book is going to be like that. To a degree, I think that is a fair comparison.

The books that stick with me the longest and have the most impact seem to be the ones that give language to things I have felt but never been able to explain. Those are the books that changed my life. I know for many guys, it will feel strange to read a book about the heart. I mean, are we just going to sit around in a circle and talk about our feelings while holding hands and crying? No.

While you are free to do that with your own time, this book is not about becoming emotionally mature or more in tune with your "feminine side." It is about unlocking the motives behind the passion and drives that God has placed in your life. Understanding the depths of your heart equips you to be the man or woman of God that he has made you to be. Growing in emotional maturity and putting words to your feelings or thoughts might be a byproduct of a well-kept heart. However, the purpose behind this book is to motivate you to become a Christian who is more drawn to Christ than anything else, even self-help books.

The problem with self-help is the first word, "self." I am going to do my best to make sure that by the end of this book, you are not inflating the self beyond what is biblical. That's a fancy way of saying, get ready to experience some humility (with me, of course!). If you apply the methods found in this book, one of the byproducts will be humility toward God and your fellow humans.

You will notice in my example of unmet expectations that I labeled selfishness as a problem in my life. Developing the skill to label your own selfishness is an incredibly powerful tool that allows you to be a Christ follower who is in the process of untangling their heart but lives from a heart that is well-fed. Here is something that has helped me when discovering my selfishness: Take a step back. Take some time and review the motives that drive you to action. Ask yourself if anyone else receives the benefit or if it's just for you. If you can see only benefits for yourself, then you know you can label your action as selfish. In my example, I want to feed my heart, but the timing is what may be selfish, not the action itself. I need to consider when might be the best time for my family, which may not be as attractive for me, but it is what will keep all our hearts well-fed.

This exercise gets tricky because it is usually not so straightforward. We will typically have to navigate some lies to get to the truth of our motives. The person we lie to the most is ourself. For example, someone has been stealing candy from my children. Despite the regular influx of candy to the pantry from events and holidays, somehow the Smarties and Butterfingers seem to disappear. "I am only taking my 'Dad Tax,'" says someone who looks a lot like me with chocolate around his mouth. The truth is, I am selfish, and I have taken something that does not belong to me. However, lying to myself and mislabeling my selfishness as a "Dad Tax" helps me not to feel guilty about stealing.

This lie is incredibly complex in my psyche compared to the relatively small amount of damage that it does. In truth, my kids are so accustomed to me stealing their candy that they don't even seem to mind anymore! It takes a lot of willpower to muster the courage to label my selfishness. It also takes a lot of humility to admit that what I have done is wrong.

A LIVING SACRIFICE

> "I appeal to you therefore, brothers, by the mercies of God, to present your bodies as a living sacrifice, holy and acceptable to God, which is your spiritual worship. Do not be conformed to this world, but be transformed by the renewal of your mind, that by testing you may discern what is the will of God, what is good and acceptable and perfect."
>
> Romans 12:1–2

One of my favorite images in Scripture is the image of the living sacrifice. If you know your Old Testament, you know that it is a reference to Abraham's willingness to sacrifice his son, Isaac. This story is familiar to those of us who grew up in the church. However, the flannelgraph version of this story has Isaac as a small boy around the age of six or seven. In reality, biblical scholars believe that Isaac was at least a teenager, if not in his twenties, when Abraham was to sacrifice him to the Lord. They believe this because Scripture tells us that it was

Isaac's responsibility to carry the wood up the mountain for the offering. The amount of wood required to burn up a goat—or a person—is significant. I know that's not a pleasant thought, but it's true. You can read about this story in Genesis 22.

What is not found in the pages of Scripture are the details of Abraham's conversation with Isaac. He likely told his son that he believed God would raise him back up from the dead (Heb. 11:19). However, this still meant that Isaac would first have to be willing to die. Isaac knew the purpose of their hike up the mountain. He knew that there was not a sacrifice. Abraham had to bind his son's arms and legs. There is no way that a one-hundred-year-old man would have been able to subdue a guy strong enough to carry the wood for the offering and hoist him up on the altar. The only logical explanation is that Isaac climbed onto the altar himself.

My wife loves the antique highchair that we have at our table. I have four kids, so it has been used a lot. Not a single kid that has been stuck in that highchair has stayed seated once they are old enough to stand. If they want to stand up, it doesn't matter what restraints we choose to use, they will find a way. Imagine the baby is now a teenager and the highchair is a bunch of rocks in a pile. That kid is going to have to choose to be up there.

A believer who loves God and is seeking to honor him is in a constant battle against himself to stay on the altar. The problem is, there is no amount of pure grit that we can muster to force ourselves to stay on the altar. Our motivation must be deeper than that. We must believe that the process of becoming like Jesus is the best chance we have at an abundant life and a well-fed heart. We have to believe that we are part of something bigger and more beautiful than ourselves or what we alone can create. We have to believe in the miracle of heart-level life change.

For me, that means actively stopping the theft of candy from my children. Now, I can still access the treats in the bucket, but I had to crawl back on the altar, humble myself before my children, and ask permission to share in what is rightfully theirs. In my relationship with my wife, that means crawling on the altar and humbly admitting that I would prefer to go fishing on a particular day and time but will work to finish the responsible tasks first and with a good attitude. It also means asking her forgiveness for my lack of transparency, my selfishness in avoiding work, and for holding a grudge. There is no limit when it comes to the sacrifice we are called to place on the altar.

CALLED TO STAND OUT

I grew up in Berean Bible Church in Knoxville, Tennessee. I was encouraged at a young age to be a leader to my friends, a mentor to younger kids, and to be discipled by older adults in the church. Everyone assumes that their upbringing is "normal," and I was no exception. It wasn't until I moved away to college that I realized just how unique my formative years were compared to the average church kid. My church life involved extensive training on matters of the heart that most people growing up in the church never receive.

For example, I once had a dear pastor and friend named Anton ask me if I could name ten men from my childhood whose marriages I could look up to and emulate. He thought it was a trick question because up to that point, with multiple decades of ministry under his belt, he had only met one person who could name ten strong marriages with which they had close personal ties. Much to his surprise, I nodded my head and said that I could name ten without a problem. Flabbergasted, he told me to start listing them. After I listed eleven or twelve couples, he stopped me and shared that most people struggle to get to five. I was able to list so many couples because they were in my church, dedicated to understanding their spiritual heart, deeply in love with Jesus, and committed to training the next generation to do the same.

From junior high through high school, I was in regular conversations with strong spiritual fathers and my own parents about spiritual matters. I did not have to go far to find someone older and wiser than myself to ask about the challenges of life, if God exists, matters of identity, theology, worldview, or whatever else concerned me at the time.

In high school, I joined an accountability group of guys my age and my youth pastor. We called ourselves Warriors, and that is exactly what we were. We engaged in spiritual warfare for each other on a weekly basis. It was not an accountability group that existed solely to shame the guy who failed with a habitual sin but to call to account and then build up our brothers in Christ—to feed each other's hearts.

Every conversation in that group was centered on the heart. It may seem weird to imagine a group of high school boys excited about opening up their hearts to each other on a weekly basis, but we were! It was warfare, but we could see change in our hearts. Some of the most powerful spiritual breakthroughs of my life happened because of that group. It started me on a lifelong journey to understand my heart and to help others understand theirs as well.

There are downsides to having grown up in this environment. Once you experience deep friendship and Christian brotherhood on that level, anything less than that feels cheap. On one occasion, I left a church that was doing good ministry because I did not have opportunities for good heart-level conversations. A friend of mine had a similar experience when he could not find deep relationships. After seeking counsel, he was told, "It seems that what you experienced in that season of time was special and unique to that church. You are likely to never find that again unless you are willing to create it yourself."

The dream I am pitching to you, dear reader, is one that will be difficult and frustrating to create. Most people cannot look past the necessary disciplines of radical honesty and vulnerability, and as a result, they will continue going through life detached from their hearts. In doing so, they are chasing a life of comfort and missing out on a life of abundance and deep relationships. Pursuing your own heart, to go deeper with God, can leave you dissatisfied with surface conversations and relationships. You will yearn for more intimacy with God and with God's people. When others do not share this vision, it can leave you feeling alone. This reality is frightening, so why would anyone unlock their heart?

FEAR STANDS IN THE WAY

"God gave us a spirit not of fear but
of power and love and self-control."

2 Timothy 1:7

Fear can grip us, can't it? I am afraid of spiders. I am afraid of being electrocuted when I have to occasionally replace a light fixture. I am afraid of drowning. All these fears are reasonable, and none of these fears are what Paul is referencing in 2 Timothy 1:7. Fear helps us to rightly understand some dangers in this life. If we did not rightly fear things of great danger like grizzly bears, we might try to pet one in the wild. This would not end well for us as they are known to be incredibly aggressive.

What Paul is referring to in 2 Timothy 1:7 is not a fear that keeps us alive, but one that keeps us from living. God has not given you a spirit that is to live fearfully. Someone who lives fearfully is a person of inaction. They have paralysis of analysis. They make pros and cons lists but never act. They certainly will never open their heart, seek to understand it, share it with another person, and begin to live out of the freedom of being fully loved and fully known by God. How would our lives look different if we could trade in our fear for power, love, and self-control? I would call that quite an improvement.

Fear can be like a one-foot wall. A one-foot wall may be anything that stands as an obstacle between us and what we desire, but it is also relatively easy to overcome. It is the paperwork at the doctor's office. They are those inconvenient things that make us work just a little bit to ensure we don't go to the doctor just because we are bored. One notable speaker had a problem with protesters. He made a one-foot wall by holding his lectures at eight in the morning. That one minor inconvenience stopped the protestors from targeting his speaking engagements.

I have found in my role as a worship leader that I need one-foot walls to act as a heart-check for those who may want to be on the stage for the wrong reasons. As I lead our church in worship, I really want to make sure that those alongside me are also willing to sacrifice, join in, and fully commit so that we learn from one another and trust one another's hearts as we minister. Leading worship can also push people to face their fears of stage fright. In this case, fear itself becomes a one-foot wall that stops a potentially good thing from happening. If we examine our hearts and find we are unwilling to follow Jesus when the only thing standing in our way is fear, we are stopped, and the enemy has a foothold. Let us not allow an insignificant obstacle like fear keep us from what God has called us to do.

I have a friend, Cameron, who worked a low-level job on the set of a TV show in Nashville. He once told me he had the lead actress's phone number. Not only that, but he was able to convince her to have lunch with him. I have heard other people describe Cameron as a man who does not fear rejection. He has since gone into sales and made quite a comfortable living for himself.

Craig Groeschel writes in his book *The Power to Change*, "You do what you do because of what you think of you." He goes on to explain: "Research shows that when making a choice, we essentially (and subconsciously) ask ourselves three questions: 1. 'Who am I?' 2. 'What kind of situation is this?' 3. 'What would someone like me do in this situation?' Your self-identity is a primary reason that you make decisions."[1] My friend Cameron has adopted the identity of a man who does not fear rejection, and it has brought him great success. What would our lives look like if we adopted the identity given to us in Scripture?

Imagine how your life would change if you identified more as a person of power, love, and self-control than a person controlled by fear. Fear stops us. That is its job. It can stop us from harming ourselves by giving us respect for things dangerous or harmful. We are even supposed to fear the Lord in reverence and recognition of his great power over all life and death. However, we are not to fear everything. When it comes to examining our own hearts and dealing with the uncomfortable things within, we are not to cave in to our fears. We are to claim our new identity.

The biggest problem with fear is when it begins to fuel the lies that we tell ourselves. "No one needs to know how much that comment about my weight stung. I probably deserve it. I have been slacking off." Fear of being known will keep every poisonous thought like this one internalized. Thoughts like this will begin to rot if they are not removed and will cause damage to us and eventually to all those around us.

Power, love, and self-control are the gifts given to us through the Spirit. Sometimes we have to preach to ourselves in the voices of power, love, and self-control. In this scenario, God's power addresses negative thought patterns with truth. Power begins, "No. That comment about my weight is broken and will not define me. I am defined by who God says I am—loved as I am—and nothing else." Love says, "The person who said this is broken on the inside and needs compassion. I will fill myself with God's love and allow that to overflow onto this hurting person." Self-control chimes in with, "This will go no further. These thought patterns are done, and I am actively placing them at the feet of Jesus at the cross. I will not respond in a similar manner but choose to speak life."

Putting on the identity of power, love, and self-control is not easy, but it does lead to an abundant life and one where we live from our spiritual heart of truth. Take the first step toward understanding your heart and confess to God that you need him to unravel fear's grip on you. Tell him that you want to be open to the benefits of being known and experience his love for you. Unlock part of your heart by putting on a new identity.

GROW UP AND BECOME A CHILD

Scripture tells us our true identity in Christ, but something strange can happen as we read. The words of 1 John 3:1 speak plainly of the Father's love for us and that we are his children. John then adds the kicker, "And that is what we are!" (NLT). We may think in our head and heart, "Yes, this is true. God loves the whole world and sent his Son to die for it, and now he loves me because he loved the world." There is nothing untrue in that thought, but it is incomplete. Having knowledge of something true does not mean that we have allowed it to drip down into our identity. This verse is about establishing our identity in our hearts.

Instead of picking out the truths and labeling them in your mind, go one layer deeper into this verse and see where it is speaking to your identity. The verse is not spewing facts. It is reminding you who you are. You are a child of the King. You are loved by him in exactly the same way that a dad loves his son or daughter. It is not just that you are allowed to pray to him because he is God and you are supposed to but that he leans down when you call his name, just like a dad does for his child when they say, "Daddy, I have a secret."

This verse is calling you to sit in wonder and awe of this truth that God identifies you as not just *a* child but *his* child. It begs the question: How do God's kids talk? How do they brush their teeth? How much of their money do they keep for themselves, and how much do they spend advancing their Father's kingdom? Do they even know who they are? Do their brothers and sisters in the faith have any clue who they are? Can they know him without knowing themselves?

Unlocking our hearts unlocks a deeper identity. It allows God to enter places of our hearts that will transform us into being more like Christ. Not just in action, because that is all on the surface. We become more like Jesus from the inside out. That is when we begin to experience a deep connection to him, radical life change, fulfillment, and the painful removal of sin from our hearts.

Father, I want to be more like Jesus, not just on the outside, but transformed deep in my heart. I want to know what it is to hold fast to a new identity and purpose for my life. Give me a passion for your Word so that I may discover more of who you have called me to be and experience the dramatic transformation that comes with a life surrendered to you. Jesus, help me to be a living sacrifice and to crawl back up on the altar so that I am giving you my best, not just what is left over. I trust that a life committed to you and the work of your kingdom is the most fulfilling life I can live. I trust you.

Amen

NOTE

[1] Craig Groeschel, *The Power to Change: Mastering the Habits That Matter Most* (Zondervan, 2023), 9, 12.

CHAPTER THREE

BAD NEWS—BETTER NEWS

I watched my breath slowly rise as my exhale created warm wisps of air like a crown around my head. Seated twenty-five feet above the forest floor, I felt a sense of royal majesty wash over me. I surveyed the land from my frigid throne, my eyes straining to see as far into the wood as possible as they systematically swept back and forth through the trees in front of me. I had taken up archery in middle school, and I was determined, now that I was a grown man with children of my own, that I would harvest a deer with a bow and arrow at least once while my children were young enough to still be impressed with their old man.

This being my first year attempting to hunt large game, I did nothing to prepare my patch of land. I just showed up early, found some tracks, climbed a tree with my stand, and began to hope for the best. I could only see roughly two hundred feet in front of me, and far less than that when the fog from my own breath filled my vision.

It is truly unsettling how quietly an animal the size of a buck can move through the forest. All 120 pounds of the young buck crept slowly through the woods to within forty feet of me without my taking notice. The natural sound it made as it took each step, the color of its fur, and even the six points on its antler rack all helped it to blend into the surrounding foliage in unassuming camouflage. My heart began to pound so loudly in my chest that I was afraid the animal would pick up the steady beat with its sensitive hearing and be scared away. Luckily for him, I gave him a far more obvious sign of danger. I tried to stand up.

The practical logistics of hunting worked out very differently from my daydreaming about hunting. My ideal plan was that I would see a deer at the edge of my visual range and have plenty of time to stand, position my bow, draw my arrow, and simply wait for the deer to present a perfect shot. Instead, the deer seemed to materialize right in front of me. I was able, with trembling hands full of adrenaline, to grab my bow, but there was no way to draw or change my position. The deer was too exposed and within range. When I should have waited for it to move behind cover, I did the opposite. I tried to stand up. I may as well have blown a bullhorn; he took off, running directly beneath my tree and one hundred yards behind my stand.

In a flash, I nocked my arrow to my bowstring, stood, and drew the bow back while also attempting to do some strange form of aerial yoga to get my body in a position where I had a chance to take a shot if he stopped running. He finally stopped to look at my tree. I considered firing an arrow on the .0001 percent chance it would find its mark (at that point, my max distance for an accurate shot with a bow was about forty-five yards), but wisdom prevailed. I have seen that same deer on my trail camera taunting me every season since this incident.

It is frustrating that I tried to stand when I should have shown some patience, that I did not have the proper clothes to keep me warm, and that I didn't see the buck until he could have spit on my tree. My biggest frustration, however, is that I didn't have an opportunity to miss the shot. You would think I would be most disappointed in failing to harvest the animal, but you would be wrong. Every whitetail hunter knows that they will miss deer, especially if they are bow hunting.

It is hard to explain just how challenging it is to shoot a bow accurately when it's cold and your body is flooded with adrenaline. I had no idea until I laid eyes on that animal that my hands would shake uncontrollably, my breathing would be labored, and my clarity of mind would fly out the window when the time came for me to act in careful, slow, and deliberate movements. It isn't something you can practice. You have to experience the thrill and dread of the moment to fully understand. In that moment, you know how easy it is to forget your hours of practice and make small mistakes that result in a missed shot. It's forgivable to take the shot and miss, but it feels downright shameful to never have the opportunity to shoot in the first place.

The Bible uses the illustration of archery a number of times. That may be one of the reasons I love the hobby so much. My favorite way the Bible talks about archery is in reference to sin. One of the common Greek words that we translate as *sin* means "to miss the mark." Every archer knows what that feels like. Long before hiking into the woods, bow hunters stand in a field and practice their craft in a controlled environment. Missing the mark is part of the learning process for archery.

WHY WE MISS THE MARK

In much the same way, missing the mark in life is how we grow and mature. Unfortunately for you and me, there is no teacher quite as effective as experience. I have little kids, so I am daily reminded that experience teaches kids faster than warnings. In fact, just yesterday I told my son that if he attacked the giant cardboard box with his homemade spear (which is nothing more than a stick with one end ground to a point from him meticulously rubbing it against the driveway in systematic, though barbaric, fashion) held far in front of him, it was likely to hit him in the stomach when he meets resistance or falls. Like I said . . . there is no greater teacher than experience.

I like this definition of sin as missing the mark. It still carries with it our traditional mindset of sin as a form of rebellion against God. That is very true! Sin *is still* rebellion against a perfect and holy God. However, it also carries a plethora of other ways that sin can cause us to miss the mark in life. Just like my experience hunting showed me that there are many factors interfering with my intentions to hit my target, this definition of sin also opens the door for an expansion of our concept of how sin makes us miss.

This concept is nothing new. In fact, the very first time that we see sin enter the story of humanity, the shockwave of that sin goes way beyond the individual act of rebellion that Adam and Eve committed against God.

Not only were the people punished for the sins they committed, but every facet of how life is sustained on this earth was changed. The basic necessities of life are food, clothing, and shelter. Remember that up until this point, God had provided the food and kept the climate of their world in such a state that they had no need of clothing or shelter. The severance of the relationship between God and man did more than change the quality of Adam and Eve's life; it went as deep as to change what was necessary to sustain life on this earth. All this, and we haven't even touched on the new and extremely painful changes to the way that new life would come into the world after the effects of sin.

I mention all of this to make this point: Missing the mark is nothing more than the natural outcome of living a life bathed in sin from birth. We can't run from it. We can't deny it. We can't work our way out of it. We were born into it. To be alive on this earth as a human is to constantly struggle against things that want to kill us. On a physical level, that is a struggle for food, shelter, and clothing. On a spiritual level, sin is trying to kill us through our hearts.

> The human heart is the most deceitful of all things,
> and desperately wicked.
> Who really knows how bad it is?
> But I, the LORD, search all hearts
> and examine secret motives.
> I give all people their due rewards,
> according to what their actions deserve.
> (Jer. 17:9–10 NLT)

That is a big problem. I, for one, don't want my tombstone to read: "Here lies Jason. . . . He was desperately wicked." I don't know anyone who will tolerate a liar in their life either. Yet this verse says that our hearts spawn despicable things, and we can't understand it because it's so good at deceiving us. No wonder we miss the mark! Part of who we are tricks us, tells us convincing lies, and hides itself so well that God himself has to go on a search and rescue mission so we can understand our motives. No wonder the fountain of our hearts spews out all manner of vile things on our lives and those around us. Thank God this is not the end of the story for the human race.

The heart described in Jeremiah 17 was an old heart, a heart of stone. God promised hundreds of years before Jesus came to Earth that though we live in a world that has been deformed by the presence of sin, our hearts can return to the way they were in the garden of Eden. To use the fountain analogy, we assume that when we are saved by Jesus, he will approach our heart fountain with masonry and plumbing equipment. We think he will renovate our hearts like he's on an HGTV restoration special. That he will make us into polished-up versions of ourselves.

Jesus is not in the business of repairing hearts but replacing hearts. He is not interested in restoration but in a surgical transplant. The moment we believe that our sin problem is bigger than we can fix, ask Jesus to save us, trust in his finished work on the cross that takes away the punishment of that sin, and believe that he rose from the dead, we are rolled out of the operating room with a new heart beating in our chests.

He alone can do the surgery because he alone is the one who hit the mark! Jesus never missed. He never failed, never sinned, and always did what the Holy Spirit told him to do. Because of his perfect life, he was the perfect sacrifice for our sin and the perfect person to give us new hearts. Does that sound dramatic? It should.

It is only through the miracle of attaining a spiritual heart of flesh that we can become wholly human. We were created to have fully functioning spiritual hearts that not only operate according to God's will but also provide space for the Holy Spirit to live in us. There is a reason why it was so easy to believe our own lies before Jesus. We were never meant to be alone. Without the Holy Spirit in our hearts, there is no defense against self-deception. But there is no room for lies in the presence of our God.

Now, I don't know much about science, but I am pretty sure that removing a heart of stone and giving us a heart of flesh is an upgrade. Not only that, but God has also given us the gift of the Holy Spirit. Part of the Godhead himself has taken up permanent residence in our hearts. The implications of this verse are wild and exciting! Your journey to understanding and guarding your heart will not be an individual activity. You alone cannot and will not uncover any of the wonderful mysteries of your heart. Only the Spirit within you can guide and direct you to true self-discovery. He will craft a journey to the deep places of your heart that will challenge you and grow your dependence on him. He will weep with you over the broken places of your old heart. He will bring you greater joy than you have ever considered possible. He is a kind and wise guide.

WHO IS RESPONSIBLE?

"**I will give** *you* a new heart, and a new spirit **I will put** within *you*. **And I will remove** the heart of stone from *your* flesh and **give** *you* a heart of flesh. And **I will put** my Spirit within *you*, and **cause** *you* to walk in my statutes and be careful to obey my rules."

Ezekiel 36:26–27—emphasis mine

Consider this passage with a dash of analysis and a pinch of critical thinking. I think you will find even more wonderful truths. You will notice that I put certain words in bold. These words are the things God says he will do. He says "I will" a total of four times in these two verses. I also italicized anything that has to do with *you* in the verses above. You will notice there are six things that happen to you.

Pop Quiz: What are you responsible to *do* in Ezekiel 36:26–27?

1. Everything
2. Nothing
3. Some things
4. Did you know that if you look closely, in the upper right-hand corner of the $1 bill you can see an owl?

The answer is . . . nothing. God does all the work. He gives us a new heart, he puts the Holy Spirit within us, he removes the heart of stone, he gives us a heart of flesh, he reaffirms that he will put the Holy Spirit in us, he will cause us to walk in his ways, and he will cause us to care to obey him. Objectively, this is incredibly unfair. He gives us all the benefits of a life with the Holy Spirit and takes all the responsibility *and* cost of equipping us for that life. Here's the point: If God is ultimately responsible for producing the good things we want flowing out of our hearts, we need to drastically change the way we approach self-development.

If God was the one to install our new hearts, then he is the one who has the best information about how they operate. I am an American. I don't like being dependent on someone else for anything, especially something that could make me look healthy or like a success to other people. I like to think I can pull myself up by my own bootstraps. I can grit my teeth and try really hard to figure out the reasons why all the pain and habitual sin that I bury in my heart hurts me and my loved ones. This doesn't work. I am not saying that all secular counseling or self-discovery tools are worthless. Quite the contrary! God has graciously revealed a lot of things about myself to me by using secular studies and books. However, there is a limit to how much benefit or long-term change I can apply through those sources. When it comes to being more like Jesus, I need the Holy Spirit.

From the rest of the Bible, we know God greatly desires that we be personally invested in a lifelong goal of becoming more like Christ. The new heart in Ezekiel 36 gives us the key to unlocking true, lasting, God-honoring growth in our hearts. If we want to become more like Jesus and grow in the knowledge of our deep hearts, we must develop a relationship with the Holy Spirit.

The Holy Spirit lives in the heart and knows every secret, pain, hidden sin, disappointment, passion, dream, and motive. There are likely things within our hearts that are too painful for us to know right now. In his wisdom, he has chosen to protect us from ourselves until we are mature enough to endure these pains. The question is, Do we trust him? It is not easy to admit that there are things we don't know about ourselves. However, if we are self-aware on any level, we know that there is more going on beneath the surface than what is easy to understand.

Spiritual depth, self-discovery, confessing and repenting of sin, healing, and our relationship with God are all intimately connected through our hearts. Simply put, we cannot grow in spiritual maturity without also growing in emotional maturity. We need to grow in self-discovery while also growing in relational wisdom. Each of these individual areas of focus finds its source in our hearts, so it is impossible to experience the benefits of a healthy heart without growing in these areas as well. The Holy Spirit, acting as the gatekeeper to our hearts as well as to our relationship with God, simply responds to our requests for access and guides us on our journey. His answer may not always come in the ways we would expect because he knows what is best for us and how best to develop holistic maturity in us.

Be warned: Accessing your heart through the Holy Spirit is not safe. While he does work all things for the good of those who love him and are called according to his purposes (Rom. 8:28), things that are good for us are not always comfortable. Anyone who works out on a regular basis will tell you that the pain of a good workout is not why they continue with this healthy pattern. The long-term delayed gratification of a healthy body motivates their good habits. In the same way, God uses pain in our hearts to create lasting spiritual maturity. Wisdom is being willing to see the long-term benefits through the pain of the moment. Trust in God's goodness rather than focusing on the present pain.

Additionally, there is an enemy seeking to thwart God's plans. We need to know that we hold within ourselves an incredible potential for advancing the kingdom of God with a healthy heart and well-examined life. It is not just our own sin and circumstances that will stand in the way of realizing that potential. We will meet both direct and indirect opposition to the revelation of our own hearts. John Eldredge, in his wonderful book *Waking the Dead*, made this point beautifully when he wrote, "The story of your life is the story of the long and brutal assault on your heart by the one who knows what you could be and fears it."[1]

If we want to fight back, a good place to start is with one of the most terrifying prayers I have ever prayed: "Lord, show me my sin." It's amazing how accommodating God is when we pray this prayer. In fact, come to think of it, I have never had him deny me this request. Asking that question reveals a heart that is willing to do the hard work of maturing. Identifying sin, confessing, repenting, and allowing God to heal our hearts from that sin is liberating. There is tremendous freedom to be found in a life unrestrained by the burdens of past sin. Every sin confessed removes a self-erected wall between ourselves and God. Do it often, and we will find a rich connection with the Holy Spirit.

HABITUAL SIN

A good place to start if we want to see God at work in our hearts is to look at any sin in our lives that we know is formed from bad habits. Habitual sin is hard to break, and I do mean *break*. Whenever I push back on bad habits, everything in me seems to prickle up like a porcupine and fight against what I know is good. It reminds me so vividly of Paul's own struggle against his flesh nature in Romans.

> I have discovered this principle of life—that when I want to do what is right, I inevitably do what is wrong. I love God's law with all my heart. But there is another power within me that is at war with my mind. This power makes me a slave to the sin that is still within me. Oh, what a miserable person I am! Who will free me from this life that is dominated by sin and death? Thank God! The answer is in Jesus Christ our Lord." (Rom. 7:21–25 NLT)

I love that. Thank God, Jesus is the answer. I can sense you asking, "But . . . how?" While the rest of this book will offer you tools to approach the coming battle against yourself, I want to give you some practical help.

First, get other people involved. I know that it is not fun to consider, but I learned 90 percent of what is in this book from a committed group of guys in my youth group. We, along with our youth leader, called ourselves Warriors because we were committed to fighting for a life of purity and obedience to the ways of Jesus. A major reason I am taking the time to write this book is because ever since I moved from that church and town, I have longed for relationships and training in the ways of the heart. The resource I long to use to teach my own children about the heart does not exist, so God has graciously allowed me to write it.

Second, I would encourage you to track your progress. I have learned a lot about staying organized with my thoughts and goals, and breaking a bad habit is a worthwhile goal. "Often all it takes to live intentionally is to pause before you proceed," says Ryder Carroll.[2] This simply means that your habits are not formed out of good intentions but out of a lack of intentionality. Bringing small forms of order to your life, even tracking simple data, can yield some amazing results with the help of the Holy Spirit.

TRAUMA

One of the most common places we see evidence of a new heart is when we deal with the fallout of another person's sin. That is called trauma. I use the term *fallout* intentionally, because the effect of another's sin on our lives will look strikingly similar to the aftermath of a nuclear attack. The initial shock of wrong done to us is incredibly painful and scarring. Often, that is where our focus is drawn, but if we are not careful, the toxic fallout following trauma can cause just as many issues for our hearts and for decades to come. It can even ruin our lives.

While this is not a book on therapy, and I am not a mental health professional, I do believe that God wants to be involved in healing us from our trauma. Jesus came so that we would have abundant life, and a large part of being able to live in abundance is freedom from the pains of our past. Sometimes that pain is obvious, but in many cases, we have attempted to ignore our pain. Like my kids sweeping Legos under a rug, we can act like something doesn't exist, but it is only a matter of time before it trips us up. Some trauma burrows itself so deeply in our hearts that we don't even remember it happening.

That sin, even though it wasn't ours, still infects our hearts. We cannot afford to ignore traumatic life experiences. Your trauma may seem small, commonplace, and insignificant, like the well-researched father wound that each of us carries to varying degrees, or your trauma could be very explicit, like a rape case made public by pregnancy, lawyers, and a courtroom. Hidden or not, easily identifiable or not, something from your past is informing and affecting your present.

Be prepared, because at some point on your journey to discover your heart, the Holy Spirit will expose some of your hurt—your trauma—and you will realize that it is manipulating your heart. Do not allow yourself to be controlled by your past simply because it is painful. That is not how God intends you to live your life. The life that he gives you through the new heart is one in which you can find healing from your trauma and freedom from its grip.

We will continue to unpack what you may find in your heart as you continue on this journey. Know that there is healing God can offer those with a heart of flesh, but in this moment, pause and thank him for the new heart that he has given you.

God, you own my heart. You are the creator and originator of my heart, and you care deeply for me. Holy Spirit, I am not going to run away from you. I am going to run toward you. I want to invite you to show me the deep places of my heart. Show me my sin, my pain, and the broken places of my heart. Show me any forms of resistance or walls I have tolerated in my heart. I know they are there because I wanted comfort more than you. Holy Spirit, please give me the strength to ask you to remove them. Grant me a new level of awareness of your presence in my life and a desire to keep the lines of communication between us open. Thank you for the freedom I have found in this new heart of flesh. Keep me hungry for more of you, Lord.

Amen

NOTES

[1] John Eldredge, *Waking the Dead: The Secret to a Heart Fully Alive*, expanded ed. (Thomas Nelson, 2016), 35.

[2] Ryder Carroll, *The Bullet Journal Method: Track the Past, Order the Present, Design the Future* (Portfolio, 2018), 63.

CHAPTER FOUR

CORONARY LUCHADOR

After finishing the last chapter, you might be under the impression that you are your own worst enemy. If that is the case, I have some good news and some bad news. The good news is that you are not your own worst enemy. While, yes, it is true that we believers carry the responsibility to manage and mitigate the effects of sin in our hearts, there are also other powers at play, and that is the bad news. While we are ultimately responsible for the presence of sin in our lives, it only takes a few pages of Scripture to see Satan's contribution to our downfall.

I feel like it is important to talk a little bit about Satan and the powers of darkness that oppose us, but before we go there, I want to make some things clear. We consume a lot of misleading information about evil powers and spiritual darkness, in movies, comics, social media, and other sources. Be careful.

It is so easy to get a cartoonish picture in our minds when we imagine the powers of darkness or to attribute too much power to our enemy and live life in fear.

Many authors much wiser than myself have dedicated a lot of time and effort to helping readers understand the power and limits of our enemy. For now, I will simply encourage you to take the reality of being opposed by spiritual forces into account when dealing with matters of the heart. Additionally, I will label all forces that would stand between you and Jesus as “the enemy.” Read your Bible and let God guide you in your journey to understand the forces of good and evil in this world. As you will see, one of the greatest mistakes we can make is to ignore the enemy.

It is unsettling to think about the dark and wicked characters that exist in the spiritual realm. I feel strongly that on your spiritual journey, it would be better for you to come to Christ out of a love for him, his grace and mercy that he offers as a gift, and the benefits of a life lived according to his will. This approach to God comes with humility and a desire to know him. I have seen so many Christians have unhealthy relationships with God and the church when they turn to God only because they are afraid to go to hell. We in the biz like to call this approach to God “fire insurance.”

I have seen many believers walk the difficult path of unpacking unhealthy assumptions about God that were not informed by Scripture but by culture and the fear of judgment. I believe unhealthy approaches to God come from someone who forgets how relational God is and falsely assumes that God is all about making cosmic legal transactions with his creations. The beauty of a life in Christ is that a legal transaction is simply part of the process that God uses to make us family. In the same way that a judge, a courtroom, and a lot of paperwork is part of the process we use to adopt a child, there is a legal transaction that occurs when we accept the free gift of eternal life offered to us by Jesus's death on the cross.

FAMILY

"You have not received a spirit that makes you fearful slaves. Instead, you received God's Spirit when he adopted you as his own children. Now we call him, 'Abba, Father.'"

Romans 8:15 NLT

I care deeply for my children, and I didn't want them to be scared into saying a sinner's prayer. I was so scared that I unintentionally left hell out of our conversations about the gospel. It wasn't until my oldest son asked me what hell was that I realized I had messed up. I wanted so much for him to love and understand how much better it was to be in a relationship with Jesus that I forgot to tell him about the downside of rejecting Jesus.

The truth is, good news only gets better when it is seen in contrast to bad news. It is not only that we are able to be adopted into God's family; it is also that we deserve eternal punishment because of the sin in our hearts. So I told my children about the reality of hell, that God is in the right to judge everyone, and that the grace we receive from Jesus is truly amazing because without it, hell is what we deserve. My kids' response to the bad news was truly beautiful. They are more concerned for the eternal destiny of their friends. As a result, it has ignited in me a sense of urgency to the gospel message that I had allowed to dwindle.

It is unsettling to think about having an enemy, but the Bible makes it clear that we have one. In fact, more than that, the Bible gives us an edge in the fight against the evil one. The

Bible gives us clues to how evil will attack our hearts. Satan is called the father of lies, the deceiver, the accuser, an adversary, an obstruction, and the opposition. So he will try to trick us, attack our identity, distract us, and otherwise try to derail any attempts we make to get closer to God. It is a huge disservice to ourselves if we ignore that which opposes us.

Imagine what it would be like if you played sports but acted like the other team did not exist. If you were the quarterback, you would get sacked every play. In basketball, you would never shoot because the other team would steal the ball. Do not ignore the enemy. We have to admit that we are opposed and identify his strategies in order to defend ourselves. Better yet, we have the distinct honor of opposing the opposer for our King.

I don't want us to feel helpless against the enemy; in fact, we have a huge advantage in the fight. The truth is, our enemy is not very creative. We know the tools he likes to use, and they are universal. Go anywhere on the globe, and we will see depression, anxiety, fear, lies, physical pain, despair, discouragement, and other unpleasant tools he uses, because again, the enemy isn't creative. Whatever the enemy is throwing at you now has been seen and overcome before through the power of Jesus, but Jesus wants you to join in the fight.

A HOUSE DIVIDED

I have the opportunity to talk to high school students on occasion, and I love to ask this question: Who said, "A house divided cannot stand." Inevitably, a large portion of the group who just walked out of an American history class will shout, "Abe Lincoln!" While he did say this iconic phrase in an attempt to keep the United States . . . well . . . united, he was actually quoting someone else.

> Knowing their thoughts, he said to them, "Every kingdom divided against itself is laid waste, and no city or house divided against itself will stand." (Matt. 12:25)

That's right, Jesus was the first one to say this iconic line. He certainly wasn't talking about the American Civil War, however, so let's take a look at why he would say that.

Let me set the scene for you. Jesus was becoming a problem for the Pharisees, the religious leaders who held a lot of power over the Jews by adding extra rules to the law of Moses. They couldn't quite figure out who or what Jesus was. What started out as probing questions about Jesus quickly turned to accusations and eventually death threats aimed at the Son of God. So the people who knew the Bible the best and who should have recognized Jesus as the promised Messiah and Savior were out to trap him in his words or actions so they could justify killing him. The problem was that Jesus, being perfect, never made mistakes.

In a desperate attempt to discredit Jesus's ministry, they began to spread rumors about him. The strategy they chose was that Jesus's power to cast demons out of people came from his association with the kingdom of darkness. That is when Jesus said that a house divided cannot stand. It is tempting to put this quote on a sign and hang it in your mom's kitchen, use it to talk about unity in the church, or quote it to emphasize the importance of teamwork on the football field. In context, however, Jesus was talking about our enemy and issuing a warning.

If our enemy hasn't fallen on its own, then we gain some valuable information about how to fight. We can clearly see that the enemy continues to deceive, destroy, and otherwise resist the advancement of the kingdom of heaven in our world, so we know that it is not divided against itself. Therefore, if the enemy is not divided, it is united around something. The question is, What unites an enemy of God?

The answer is *honor*. Anything that honors God, gives glory to God, or even has the potential to bring honor to God is a massive threat to our enemy. Think about it: When Lucifer fell, it was because he felt that he deserved God's glory and praise. He wanted the honor of being God. When he deceived Eve, he tempted her with her desire to "be like God." This simply reveals that she wanted to be worthy of honor apart from God.

BACK TO THE HEART

You may be asking yourself why we are spending so much time learning about the enemy in a book that is all about the heart. It is so you can be prepared to face the enemy's strategy and motives. I mentioned at the beginning of this chapter that you are not your own worst enemy, that there are evil forces at play in the battle for your heart. This chapter serves as a warning to you that you will enter some fights as you grow in spiritual and emotional maturity in your heart. However, God has given you tools through Scripture to be able to fight the enemy and see victories.

I think that sometimes we read passages like Ezekiel 36 with its new heart of flesh or John 3 when Nicodemus asks Jesus about being born again, and we assume that because God is the one who produces new life within us, he will just magically make us pure and whole. Then when the enemy's schemes work on us, we are discouraged and stop our forward progress. Unfortunately for many people, the slightest resistance to a good thing is enough to keep them from keeping up the fight.

I know that you are not one of these people because you have made it to the fourth chapter of this book. You have resisted the urge to hop on Instagram and doomscroll, and you have chosen to better yourself and your understanding of how your heart fits into the rest of your life by picking up a book. Most people give up at the slightest resistance to their goals. In fact, some studies show that as many as 33 percent of New Year's resolutions are abandoned during the first week of January.[1]

Everyone has their downfalls when attempting to overcome resistance. Some people have no problem working out every day but struggle to have difficult conversations with their loved ones. Others choose challenging careers but are flabbergasted by the thought of the particular difficulties that come with raising children. When it comes to fighting for our hearts, however, we cannot afford to take the easy way out and ignore our problems.

DISCOURAGEMENT

Getting us to avoid the fight for our hearts is the primary attack the enemy will use on us. All the enemy has to do to stop us from making progress is discourage us. We will experience a personal breakthrough, feel emotional and spiritual clarity and purpose, and then someone will question our motives, our dog will die, or we will go through a breakup, and all the good things will stop. It doesn't matter what form the discouragement takes. Even a slight hint of discouragement can seriously derail the good thing that God began in us.

My fellow worship leaders know about this phenomenon from personal experience. It is not uncommon that I will plan a Sunday service with a lot of songs that I know will move people in the congregation. The service will go off without a hitch, and people will seriously respond to the presence of God. I will be on cloud nine because of the powerful moments that God allowed me to be a part of creating in the room. After the service, when I am still overwhelmed by what God has done, one person can come to me with a complaint and deflate the moment entirely. Ninety-nine people could compliment me on doing my job well, but one critic can undo it all.

This certainly is not right, and it is not the way that God wants us to live. I am simply pointing out that if we are not prepared to resist the attack of discouragement toward our hearts, we are vulnerable to the enemy's attacks. Defense looks a lot like resilience, emotional maturity, and spiritual maturity. All those things are developed in our spiritual hearts. The enemy just wants us to stop.

Most of the time, the enemy's goal is not to turn us into devil worshipers with one swish of a magic wand. The enemy's goal is first to stop us from bringing honor to God. Being spiritually and emotionally equipped to handle these basic attacks is a huge threat to the enemy. Remember that the enemy is not sophisticated in its attack, but that is because most people are not thinking about their need for a defense.

THE OFFENSIVE

"Humble yourselves before God. Resist the devil, and he will flee from you. Come close to God, and God will come close to you. Wash your hands, you sinners; purify your hearts, for your loyalty is divided between God and the world."

James 4:7–8 NLT

When I think of resisting, I think of a defensive posture. Do not miss that resisting in this context causes the enemy to run. There is something about resisting that is an offensive attack on the enemy. I know I have written a lot about our own failings and the enemy that is against us, but I never want us to feel like we can't win. This verse is telling us that if we are humble before God, if we depend on him for our strength and trust that he will guide us on the journey to living out of the reality of the new heart he has given us, all we have to do is show a little resistance to the enemy and he will turn tail and run. He runs because true resistance to discouragement or any of the other attacks he may hurl against us is proof of God at work inside us. We are intimidating to the enemies of the kingdom of heaven when we walk with Jesus.

Following the instruction to resist the devil, James sums up in two commands *how* he expects us to resist. We will start with the second command. He says we have to make a choice between God and the world. Clearly, this is the overarching battle between good and evil. It does no one any good to try to ride the fence, so make a decision for God and stick to it.

The first command is to purify our hearts. As we grow in emotional and spiritual maturity, we will also grow in purity. God is in the business of making us more like himself, and he is completely pure. I should also mention that this is another powerful way we can resist the enemy. Growing in purity removes areas where the enemy can grab on to pull us down and discourage us.

So, we have determined to prove our loyalty to God, to work on becoming pure like Jesus, and to resist the enemy. This all sounds wonderful until we attempt to put some of these concepts into practice in life. That discouragement thing is really a bear, and we certainly cannot expect to be 100 percent optimistic to the point of being unrealistic about life. Now is the point where we lace up some boxing gloves and prepare our hearts for conflict.

CONFLICT

I do not like conflict. Some people thrive on the stuff, but I am not one of them. You may not get that impression from my writing or my public speaking. I love to be well-researched and confident when I have a message to deliver. Put me in an awkward social situation, however, and I may go so far as to accept blame for wrongs I did not commit just to cool another person's temper. The strange thing is, once I am totally cornered, the fight doesn't last long.

My dad is a black belt. I had the distinct privilege of being around a lot of martial arts training as a young lad. While never quite getting to black belt status myself, I did climb the ranks a bit, certainly enough to learn this lesson: real fights don't last long. Much to my chagrin, real life does not mirror action movies. A quick Google search makes it clear that most street fights are in the range of twenty to thirty seconds long, with a general consensus that a fight lasting more than sixty seconds is a long one.[2]

However, being married has taught me that some fights last for days! I guess that when words are thrown instead of fists, it's much harder to land a knock-out blow. The rules of engagement are also far less defined, so anything and everything becomes a target. Honestly, I can't decide which version of fighting I would prefer. They are both just terrible to go through.

I am so thankful that I have never had to use my martial arts training in the real world. I am also thankful that it gives me an edge to end fights quickly, or better yet, to de-escalate them before they begin. I am even more thankful that I was trained from a young age to understand and fight for my heart. It has completely transformed how I communicate with other people, the way that I recognize and deal with my sin, how I humbly call out sin in others, and how I see long-term spiritual growth in my life.

You too can fight for your heart. You are called to wrestle with your heart. Specifically, the part of your heart that wants to go back to the way things were before Jesus. The Bible calls this part of you the flesh. It is a struggle, and there is conflict. No one is particularly thrilled to dive into a fight. It takes courage and tenacity. Most importantly, it takes faith that there is victory on the other side of the fight. I think that is the missing piece most Christians forget. We put our heads down and plow forward in our self-improvement, all the while knowing that we will never really "arrive."

That's the reality of our situation. We know and deeply love the truth of Ezekiel 36 and our new heart of flesh with the Holy Spirit living with us, and yet we know that perfection on this side of heaven is out of our reach. The old patterns of our sinful flesh remain even though our sinful nature was removed along with our old heart. Reaching this conclusion felt like a crisis moment for me until I started to see similar situations everywhere in life. This is what I like to call living in tension.

TENSION

Think about a person you love dearly in this world. Not someone you have a crush on or someone you have been in love with for less than two years, but someone you love who has been in your life for a long time. A parent or sibling is a great option. Think about how much you have caused that person pain through your words, decisions, or actions. Is it not strange that this person you love is also the person you regularly hurt the most? The more time you spend with someone you love, the more you will hurt them. This is the kind of tension I am talking about.

There are plenty of other examples of living in tension. We have to tear our muscles in order for them to grow. Sharpshooters know that "slow is smooth, smooth is fast." We want fame and the famous want privacy; we don't know what we have until it is gone; we can die from not eating enough or eating too much, and the list goes on. If we are willing to look closely, we will notice that life in tension is one of the consequences of living in a world that has been twisted by sin. God's expectation is that we will live and thrive while also living in this world full of naturally occurring tensions.

Paul wasn't happy about it either. In Chapter Three, we read his famous discourse on the tension between what he wanted to do and what he actually did as a result of the sin in his heart. Paul understood the tension. In a way, it is comforting that a major contributor to the Scriptures knows and mourns the same struggle that we face today. I have certainly felt like the more I focus on not sinning, the faster I cave to sin. If I am honest, I have also had my fair share of moments when I felt dominated by sin, was miserable with myself, and just wanted to give up. Remember, I hate conflict. I think the worst conflict is inner conflict, the same battle that Paul was fighting. The old patterns of the flesh are familiar to us, and it is easy to slip into them without even being conscious that we are doing it again. Sin grows and grows until addressing it is inescapable. The worst version of feeling trapped is when we know that we have trapped ourselves.

So what are we supposed to do? When we reach the end of ourselves and don't like what we see? Paul gives us truth to hold on to and explains why it is worth it to fight for our hearts:

> Now there is no condemnation for those who belong to Christ Jesus. And because you belong to him, the power of the life-giving Spirit has freed you from the power of sin that leads to death. (Rom. 8:1–2 NLT)

The truth is that sin no longer has power over you. When God looks at you, there is no condemnation or disappointment. He just sees Jesus and his righteousness. The first step in fighting for your heart is to remember that the battle is already won.

I think most people, including myself, get tripped up on the concept of being saved by Jesus but still living with evidence of sin in their lives. This passage really helps to clear up that sticky situation. While we live on this earth, we are capable of falling back into the fleshly patterns of sin, but because of Jesus, we are free from the *power* of sin.

For some reason, that makes me think of the classic imagery of a flower growing in a landfill. Jesus removes the power of sin from our hearts, showing a glimmer of hope and evidence of amazing things to come. In these moments when we see the power of sin eradicated in our hearts, we begin to operate in my favorite form of tension, the "now and not yet."

This tension is my favorite because ultimately it is a fight for our true identity. Your heart defines who you are, and God has given you a new heart, but at the same time, you have to fight to live out of the new life he has given you. Paul again defines our state of tension so well.

> I don't mean to say that I have already achieved these things or that I have already reached perfection. But I press on to possess that perfection for which Christ Jesus first possessed me. No, dear brothers and sisters, I have not achieved it, but I focus on this one thing: Forgetting the past and looking forward to what lies ahead, I press on to reach the end of the race and receive the heavenly prize for which God, through Christ Jesus, is calling us. (Phil. 3:12–14 NLT)

We will never "make it" on this side of eternity. That is not the promise of a new heart from God. We will never reach full perfection. In fact, perfectionism itself can turn into a massive form of discouragement on our spiritual journey. However, there is good reason to fight, to run the race, to press on, and to keep working on becoming more like Jesus. We have a heavenly prize awaiting us at the finish line. Jesus himself is the prize. We don't win the race by trying harder or life-hacking our way to purity but by claiming our eternal status as coheirs with Christ. That reality gives you the strength to put in the work. I pray that you are inspired to press on with the work that needs to be done in your heart. In the next two chapters, we will go deeper into our hearts to discover how God transforms us from the inside out and equips us with all we need to run the race.

God, I pray that from your glorious, unlimited resources, you will empower me with inner strength through your Spirit, and that I will be well-equipped and well-disciplined to run with endurance the race before me. Jesus, be my guide and trainer as you prepare me to fight the good fight of faith to win back my heart. Strengthen and inspire me through the Holy Spirit to understand who God made me to be. Grant me the courage to fight for purity and the tenacity to resist the enemy.

Amen

NOTES

[1] John C. Norcross and Dominic J. Vangarelli, "The Resolution Solution: Longitudinal Examination of New Year's Change Attempts," *Journal of Substance Abuse* 1, no. 2 (1988–89): 127–34, https://doi.org/10.1016/S0899-3289(88)80016-6.

[2] Gregory Knapp, "Facts You Should Know about Street Fighting," Self Defense Guides, December 19, 2023, www.selfdefenseguides.info/street-fighting/facts-you-should-know-about-street-fighting.html.

SECTION TWO

CHAPTER FIVE

DETECTIVE WORK

It was the perfect crime. Not a soul stirred in the stillness of the house. The steady hum of ceiling fans obstructed what would otherwise have been incriminating noises coming from the kitchen. The children usually sleep heavily, but there seems to be another level of depth that affects slumber only at six in the morning. While their eyes darted behind closed eyelids, deep in REM sleep, there was a rustling in the pantry. When they finally wake, they will find a bag, half-empty, that used to be sealed and filled to the brim with Sour Patch Kids.

I am their most likely suspect because it is a documented fact that I will eat anything with sugar near the top of its ingredients list. This alone is no proof, but it's certainly known that I have the means to take the candy. The means is simply the ability plus proximity required to do the crime. It is also no secret that I love Sour Patch Kids, so they have me pegged for motive. This would not be the first time I have eaten candy in secrecy.

Having the means and the motive make for a strong case, but not enough to prove my guilt. It is not until I am betrayed by the faint traces of sweet and sour dust on my pajamas that my guilt is confirmed by the addition of evidence.

I don't know much about being a detective. I don't know that I have spent any time with a real detective in my life. In fact, I am realizing now that most of what I know of detective work comes from buddy-cop comedies and my deep love of Sir Arthur Conan Doyle's short stories. While I seriously doubt that any self-respecting detective today would don a deerstalker hat and smoke a meerschaum pipe like Sherlock Holmes, I do find from my own observation of the profession that they are all after the same three things. In order to prove their case, a detective needs to convince the judge and jury with evidence that the suspect had the means and motive to commit the crime.

This is a silly (and possibly true) example of just how important those three elements are for exposing wrongdoing. What you will do over the course of the next two chapters is use these tools on yourself to see what you can uncover about your heart. In Chapter Four, the reality of the fight before you and the partnership you have with Christ was the focus. Now it is time to lace up the boxing gloves and throw some punches at the enemy by removing the places in your heart where there is proof that he has gained a foothold.

There is one key difference between accusing a criminal and using means, evidence, and motive to understand and uncover broken places of our hearts, and that is the strength of each element. In a courtroom, evidence is king. Cold cases cannot be reopened after a period of time unless new evidence is found. Evidence is so powerful that too much can make something look like a setup, and a lack of evidence can get you laughed out of the courtroom with the case dismissed. In matters of the heart, evidence does not hold the same kind of weight. We will look at it in a practical light in this chapter, but the fountain analogy in Chapter One resonates because it tells us what we already know—that evidence and the means to do wrong exist in our lives and are out of control. Motive is the key ingredient that lurks in the shadows of our hearts.

DETECTIVE

In the last chapter, we discovered that not only are we sometimes at odds with ourselves but also that there is a manipulative and highly tricky enemy against us. Pair those together, and it can begin to feel overwhelming. It is like an obstacle course that sets itself up to slow us down on our journey from who we are today to who God is calling us to be tomorrow. We know that we need to keep pushing forward and clawing through each stumbling block, but from our viewpoint on the starting line, it is hard to know where to begin. We want to fight, to run the race well, but how do we punch an opponent we can't see?

I love this part of the journey, not because of the challenges but because what God calls us to do to push back against the darkness and reclaim our hearts is beautifully practical. This is the intersection between theory and action. Up until this point, I have attempted to convince you that God has a better life for you and you can begin to access that better life now. Before I give you the tools you need, I must issue a warning to you. The world might look at the skills you learn in the following chapters and reduce these practices to churchy gimmicks for self-discovery and self-improvement. Nothing could be further from the truth.

What God wants to do through you, he wants to do with you. You are neither the originator nor the motivator behind your spiritual and emotional growth. God wants you to be a whole person, a true human in every respect, and he is going to be your guide to becoming that person. I can't stress this enough: God has more information on you and what makes you come alive than you do. Looking at the big picture of Scripture, the trajectory of a believer's life moves toward spiritual maturity, emotional maturity, relational maturity, and purity. So fighting back against the enemy will look like God-activated growth in those areas. Fighting back is getting results that make you more like Jesus.

Heart maturity spills over into life change and is also an attack on the kingdom of darkness. What I mean is that the benefits of heart intentionality directly affect us but also go beyond us and matter deeply to the kingdom that God is building through each believer. If we want to change the world, we don't simply change ourselves. We change our hearts. If we want to fall more in love with the gospel so we will share it with others, we must allow the gospel to work on us. If we want to influence our families to be a powerful force for good and God's kingdom, we first allow that same kingdom to establish itself deeply in our hearts. Our heart change precedes and motivates us to action. However, there are some actions we can take to help the truth of who God created us to be sink into our hearts and take root.

THE MEANS

I mentioned earlier that the means is the ability plus the proximity to the crime. When we are looking at the heart, it is easy to see where we have the ability to cave to temptation. If we have a general awareness of our faults and weaknesses, it is not hard to connect the dots between what brings us shame today and what we could do to bring ourselves even more shame tomorrow. That is simply how the enemy works. Anyone who has told a white lie knows that it can grow and get out of control rapidly. We have the potential for even more harm than we may be willing to admit to ourselves at this moment.

Do not let this plunge you into despair. God uses everything, the good and the bad, to work out his will for our lives. That means that even the potential we have to commit horrible things, he uses for his good. The first time I heard the song "Glorious Day" by Passion, I knew that my church needed to sing it. I had attended a number of Passion conferences and knew that my small church of two hundred in Dalton, Georgia, would not create the same kind of atmosphere that I felt in the arena. I thought about why that might be. I realized that what I wanted to experience in my little church was not the bigness of a stadium worship service but the fresh appreciation for what the cross and resurrection mean for those who believe. No new truths, but new feelings of gratitude flooded my heart as I worshiped with this song. I wanted my whole congregation to feel that same appreciation for Jesus with me.

Rather than preach before singing the song or trying to generate some kind of emotional stirring in the congregation, I simply took my band through an exercise to help them remember the beauty of the salvation story. I gave them each a slip of paper and a pencil and asked them who they would be today without Jesus. As vividly as they could imagine, they were to write down a few of their faults, harmful character traits, or addictive tendencies and guess the person that they would have been if Jesus had not intervened in their lives. I had them write with as raw and vulgar language as they felt necessary to match the reality of who they would be without Christ. It worked. Because the band had a fresh reminder of Jesus's love for them, the church caught on as well. It wasn't just a new song. It became a new anthem for that season of our church.

This exercise can be helpful, but it is not a replacement for getting to know people with testimonies that are different than our own. I don't think I ever truly understood 1 Corinthians 10:13—where it says, "No temptation has overtaken you that is not common to man"—until I rubbed shoulders with people very much like myself who had their early lives decimated by the same core temptations that plague my own life. There is no title or life achievement, such as becoming a pastor or a parent, that automatically changes a person. Those things in no way remove any temptation to sin from the heart. It is the root system of sin in my heart that manifests problems, large and small.

JESUS UNCOVERS THE MEANS

Jesus knew that recognizing sin was not the only problem humanity faced. In fact, there is a case to be made that hidden sin leads to just as much, if not more, harm as blatant rebellion against God. It is the friend who is closest to us who has the potential to do us the most harm. The same principle works in other areas of life as well. That is why people say it is wise to never meet our heroes. We inflate those we respect to be superhuman, and when they don't meet our expectations, we are personally offended.

That does not hold true with Jesus. He is exactly as advertised in the Bible, and the Bible has a lot to say about him. This includes the fact that he was there and involved in the creation of you.

> Christ is the visible image of the invisible God.
> He existed before anything was created and is supreme over all creation,
> for through him God created everything

> in the heavenly realms and on earth.
> He made the things we can see
> and the things we can't see—
> such as thrones, kingdoms, rulers, and authorities in the unseen world.
> Everything was created through him and for him.
> He existed before anything else,
> and he holds all creation together.
> (Col. 1:15–17 NLT)

When I tell you that Jesus knows you better than you know yourself, I am not just saying that as a way to comfort or motivate you. The Bible itself is very in-your-face about the fact that Jesus is involved and invested in who you are and who you will be. The question is, Are you involved and invested in who you are and who you will be? I certainly am, and this is how God has helped me in this battle. There are two practical strategies Scripture calls us to use to combat our potential for sin that we have called the means to sin.

The first is resisting the internal ability or potential for sin in our hearts. There are countless stories of people coming to Jesus and immediately being healed of their addictions to pornography, drugs, alcohol, and even cigarettes. These, however, are only the stories we hear about because they are uncommon. Everyone has a vice, and you likely did not have the desire for the sinful or unhealthy thing removed from your heart the moment Jesus took up residence.

I want to be clear that just because you likely did not experience something miraculous in an instant does not mean that God is unable or unwilling to work a miracle in your heart. More than this, there is no reason why a miracle is required to happen in an instant. The miracle that he most commonly works in the hearts of those who belong to him is that we begin to feel bad when we fail. This doesn't sound miraculous, but consider this.

The nature of sin is to hurt us and those around us. The nature of habitual sin is that it will harm us most of all. Our bodies and minds are resilient but will not stand abuse over the long term. That means that given enough time and repetition, our hearts grow calluses. Like a guitarist's fingers, our hearts can harden, losing the ability to feel pain and guilt from habitual sin. This is why those addicted to pornography often find themselves consuming content that is more and more vile as time goes on. It is the natural progression of the heart to want the same emotional stimulation it got with the first physical experience. The damage pornography causes to the heart is rarely a consideration.

On entering the heart full of calluses, the Holy Spirit will begin to peel them away. We might not recognize it at first, but guilt is a gift from God. I want to be careful here to clarify that guilt is good, but shame is not. Guilt is the bad feeling we get that makes us run to God, but shame is guilt that has been twisted into lies that we believe about ourselves. Shame is allowing our mistakes to define who we are, and only God can tell us who we are. Guilt pushes your heart toward freedom, but shame puts it in a prison.

We want to feel. We want to hurt when we mess up. It is the Spirit's way to nudge us back to the Father, back to forgiveness, and back to acceptance. If we recognize that we don't feel, that we are numb, we need to ask God to restore our ability to feel guilt for our sin. Often that is the beginning of the slow miracle we have been praying for.

The other strategy for resisting the means to sin in our lives is related to proximity. Sometimes, to remove ourselves from the proximity of temptation literally means: Run.

> Run from anything that stimulates youthful lusts. Instead, pursue righteous living, faithfulness, love, and peace. Enjoy the companionship of those who call on the Lord with pure hearts. (2 Tim. 2:22 NLT)

The same rule for real estate applies to fighting temptation, especially sexual sin. It's all about location. If we knowingly put ourselves in compromising situations and then attempt to live in purity, we are kidding ourselves and setting ourselves up for failure.

It doesn't have to be sexual in order to be damaging. If our relationship with food is unhealthy, our location and the location of our vices matter. If we put people around us as often as possible who are committed to our success, we are going to find it much easier to get the results we are looking for.

In my case, I knew that I had the potential in my heart for either something amazing for God's kingdom or something devastating for myself and those around me. I knew that I wanted to surround myself with people who were on mission to see me grow in Christ. I gave up the opportunity to build up cash at a summer job to take an internship at my church. I scrubbed toilets and did other janitorial duties in order to save up a few hundred dollars to live off of at school. I never considered these decisions to be a sacrifice but an investment in myself. The most important thing to me was to be connected to Jesus from my heart, and I needed to be physically close to spiritual mentors to help me.

EVIDENCE

This leads us to the second thing that a detective needs in order to convict a criminal: the evidence. I won't spend much time on what this looks like in your life because we have already covered this with the fountain analogy. Evidence and wrongdoing are intimately linked, and we don't need much help to find our own faults. All I will add is that evidence of sin in your life that others can see is God's way of pointing a spotlight on the places in your heart that he wants to deal with first. The evidence is useful. In addition to this, you can use evidence practically to show you how God is working out his good plan for his glory and for your good.

This whole process of uncovering sin, dealing with it, exposing it, restoring our hearts, and living a fuller life in Christ is not something we can do in a day. It is not something to be tracked or tallied. It is not even something we will be able to master in our lifetimes. The ten-thousand-hour rule does not apply to spiritual heart maturity. The beauty of the way God made us is that we never arrive at heart perfection. Remember that while the sinful nature is nailed to the cross, we still have to deal with the sinful patterns of our flesh.

This may feel discouraging initially, but let me see if I can convince you that there is true joy to be had in the journeying. As I mentioned earlier, there is beauty in the fact that God's miracles do not have to happen instantaneously for them to be miraculous. It is through this slow and steady progression to Christlikeness that we can fall deeply in love with Jesus. It is examining the evidence of sin in our lives that leads us to the revelation of all that he has been quietly working in our lives over the long term.

Going through a minor crisis earlier this year, I found that I was approaching Jesus in the same way that I would approach a best friend. (This is significant for any millennial; just ask one!) We crave deep and meaningful relationships, and I have often struggled with treating my time with Jesus as an operational or transactional relationship. Imagine my surprise when the evidence surrounding my interactions with him revealed that he is my best friend! I have longed for friendship with Jesus my whole life. I was not comfortable with the idea, and some cheesy albeit well-meaning Christian songs had twisted the concept of friendship with Christ to something that I didn't recognize as desirable. But God has a way of demolishing our unfounded and preconceived ideas about who he is, and I couldn't be more thankful.

Evidence collected over a number of years pointed me to this revelation. I doubt that I would have been able to identify my feelings and actions in my relationship with God as what they really were in the moment without that evidence. The problem is that revelations like this are not in your face. We tend to coast through life and forget to look back at what we have been through and what God is teaching us through our past. Evidence is not useful unless it is uncovered. The practical application for those who want to use the evidence of sin and their victories over sin is intentional reflection. We must be willing to process through our past in order to learn from it.

There are a number of ways to do this. Some people have found journaling to be beneficial, while others pursue counseling, jogging, coffee with a friend, or dedicated quiet times of prayer. There are many more valid examples, but I list these because they are the methods I personally have used to make breakthroughs by examining the faults and wins of my past. There is no one-size-fits-all method for examining our past. However, I will argue that involving other people in the examination process is necessary. Even when I have a breakthrough while running or working out, I will still take the time to process my life with a trusted friend, my wife, or another pastor. We need other people. We specifically need other people who are willing to listen to us.

My wife and I process life very differently. I have to get my mouth moving in order for an original thought to surface. I talk through everything. It is like my brain unlocks itself for the possibility of a breakthrough if I am asked good questions and have to answer. She, on the other hand, processes everything internally. She wants to know the questions beforehand and will sit with them marinating in her mind and heart for a long time before she is ready to give an answer. This way of processing life is just as valid as my way of processing. The end result is the same: We both grow and we do it through good communication and a willingness to listen to each other.

One of the greatest benefits of examining evidence in our lives is narrowing our focus on the things that God created us to accomplish. If we identify a failure in our past, we can turn it over and uncover what went wrong. If it boils down to an active act of rebellion toward God in our hearts, confess, repent, and move on. However, sometimes God allows failure in our lives to give us a course correction. Examining evidence can be a good way to identify that, for example, if we continue at our job, our feelings of discontentment will grow and we will become bitter. It may show us that what we thought was a healthy relationship is actually draining us emotionally or distracting us spiritually.

In a positive direction, evidence can point us to the callings, relationships, and experiences that are the most life-giving to us. Eric Liddell famously said in *Chariots of Fire*, "God made me fast. And when I run, I feel his pleasure." This is a great place to start. Of course, it takes wisdom and discernment to make sure that we aren't limiting ourselves by only doing what makes *us* happy. That is not the goal. In fact, most people who spend their lives chasing their own pleasure end their lives with the most regrets. The goal is to find what ignites our passion that aligns with God's will for our life. Take some time to look back over your past year and ask yourself where you felt like God was most pleased with you. This practice is a way of examining the evidence of his gifts in your life.

One of the most significant lightbulb moments for me as a young adult came when I met with my lifelong pastor and mentor, Pastor John Stone. Our conversation centered on the difficult realities that come with choosing a career in the church. Church work, and specifically pastoral work, can be very challenging, and he wanted me to be aware that the path I was taking was not going to be easy. He was right. He also told me that despite the hardships facing pastors, if God had called me to that role, there would be fulfillment and joy to be found in that career. He was right again.

Of course, this makes us wonder: How do we know what we are called to do? Pastor Stone's answer to this question was the same one that I offer to you, and I love the way he explained it to me. He said, "If God is good, and if he has created you for a specific purpose, doesn't it make sense that he designed you to get the most enjoyment out of the thing that he has called you to do?" Find the things that make you come alive. Examine the evidence surrounding your life and what you are specifically equipped to do and enjoy. Ask the Lord if he is pleased with your efforts. It is when you land in this place of mutual joy that you begin to make an impact on this world for God.

God, help me to be more like Jesus. Let me see clearly my constant need for your grace and mercy. Help me know the extremes of who I would be without you to propel me into deeper relationship and connection with you. Thank you that I am not who I would be without your intervention. Show me what makes you smile. Like the high priestly blessing, show me the things that turn your face and your blessing toward me. Give me joy and a purpose that honors you and advances your kingdom here on the earth.

Amen

CHAPTER SIX

WHY ASK WHY?

Sweat rolled down my forehead and into my eyes. I desperately wanted to wipe it away, but my arms were otherwise occupied. Straining against the metal bar in my hands, I just closed my eyes and kept pressing. When it felt like all the strength in my arms was gone, I imagined pressing the back of my shoulders into the bench below me. The world slowed down, and all I could think about was pushing the bar. Shaking, the bar slowly rose until my arms were fully extended. Much to my disappointment, Josh, my roommate, yelled out with Spartan energy in the small gym, "One more!"

I looked up at the bar. It was void of weights. We started with three repetitions close to my maximum weight and slowly worked our way down to just lifting the bar. Trust me, it is much more challenging than you would think. "What would someone think if they saw me struggling to lift the bar with no weights on it?" That was all I could think about as I consigned myself to another repetition. I lifted the naked bar until I couldn't lift it anymore.

The day had started like most of my college days. I was possibly out of place as a musical theater major who chose to room with rugby players. However, I knew that they would push me to my limits, and that is what I wanted from my friends. Most days, I would find myself being asked by one of them, "Want to go lift heavy things?" and I would. The results spoke for themselves. I ended the semester in the best shape of my life. That is one of the many things I wanted during that season of my life, but simple physical fitness was not motivation enough to keep me in the gym. I needed a motive that was not shallow.

Possibly when you hear the word motivation, you think of a high school football coach's halftime speech or a YouTube motivational video with some guy with a deep voice telling you to get off the couch and do something with your life while cinematic images of people sweating scroll across the screen. That is where my mind drifts at the first mention of the word. However, my motives for working out were multifaceted. I wanted to get in shape, but that was a superficial motivation. Any health and fitness guru will tell you that being motivated only by how you will look in six months is not enough to keep you going to the gym. To do hard things, you need to find a deeper purpose that will drive you through the hardship.

In my case, that deeper motive was my upcoming wedding. I wanted to enter marriage, the greatest adventure of my life, in the best shape of my life. In addition to this, working out with friends added another level to my motives. It was a chance to connect with my friends over a shared challenge on a weekly or even daily basis before my time was significantly restricted by moving off campus with my wife. The point is, when I look back at my life and the seasons when I was able to make the most progress or be consistent in healthy practices like lifting or running, there is never one key motive that kept me going. There are layers upon layers of motives that kept me waking up early, putting on tennis shoes, picking a podcast, driving to the gym, and doing the work consistently.

A TWO-WAY STREET

Motivation is a two-way street. It works for us, but it can also work against us. In the last chapter, I showed that the potential we have for great acts of rebellion toward God is substantial and that the evidence we find from our past failures and successes can help us clearly identify where God is leading us today. A good detective knows that they can always uncover the means, the evidence, and the motive behind a crime. The best way for us to know who we are created to be and to live in the fullness of our God-given calling is to do some detective work on our hearts. I also said that where evidence is king in the courtroom, motive is king of our hearts.

This might be the most important chapter of this book. If we can master the art of capturing our superficial motives and work backward to find the deeper layers of motives within our hearts, it can lead us to the biggest breakthroughs of our lives and launch us into spiritual and emotional maturity. This is the ultimate hack when it comes to knowing ourselves, our true selves.

You might be wondering why you haven't learned a lot about this spiritual practice. If knowing your motives is so powerful, then why aren't more people talking about the benefits of uncovering them? Because it can be uncomfortable. In fact, I will wager that in your mind, you could agree with everything I wrote about your heart being capable of wickedness beyond what you have acted upon in your life. However, when you unearth the motives of your heart, you begin to *feel* what it meant when God told Cain, "Watch out! Sin is crouching at the door, eager to control you. But you must subdue it and be its master" (Gen. 4:7 NLT). (*Spoiler alert!* Cain commits the first murder immediately after God tells him this.) Everything within you will be violently opposed to uncovering the motives behind your insecurities, hidden sin, and comfort, or your motives connected to trauma, addictions, and all the sin-related building blocks that make up your least-favorite parts of who you are.

Remember, the goal is not to become more of who you are but to become more like Jesus. To take the broken places of your heart and allow him access to them for your good and his glory. Uncovering these motives opens you up for an encounter with Jesus. He can do powerful work in your heart if you are willing to give him your deep motives. Jesus always has permission to invade your heart. He is sovereign and all-powerful, so there is nothing keeping him from snapping his fingers and working big things in and through you, regardless of whether you feel like you are ready for him to do the work. However, he is also all-wise, and he knows that lessons learned through experience and effort are the ones that stick. I believe that Jesus doesn't just transform us instantaneously because we benefit more from going through the process of heart transformation if we are involved in the process. So take a moment even now and ask him to be a part of this process. You can trust him to be kind to you and to lead you to the places in your heart that need his healing touch.

HOW?

There are many ways to discover yourself. I want to restate that I love personality tests, counseling, meeting with a pastor, accountability groups, and therapy. I know that each of these unique processes has led me or those close to me to significant breakthroughs. However, each of these paths is after the same thing: a deeper understanding of who you are and how you work that you can use to change your life.

The best way we can move toward that goal is by asking why. Why do we do what we do? Why do we feel how we feel? Why do we dress how we dress? Why do we pursue the same kinds of relationships over and over? Why do we trust the people we trust? Why do we go back to destructive behaviors? Each of these questions could lead us one tier closer to discovering more about ourselves or exposing sin in our hearts.

Asking why is incredibly powerful. As a parent of young children, I know it can be exasperating to continue to answer that question. My son Wyatt is incredibly curious. He is not afraid to ask good why questions if he does not understand. In fact, he regularly asks such potent *why* questions that our children's director at church recently confessed to me that some of his Sunday school teachers are nervous calling on him for fear that he will ask a theological question they are unequipped to answer. He is using the question to grow in understanding, and a lot of the time, he gets what he wants. You can do the same thing. You can use the question why to grow in understanding yourself, and it will help you get what you want.

The rest of the world has latched onto the power of the question why. Simon Sinek's book *Start with Why* is essential reading, in my opinion, for every burgeoning entrepreneur, and the principle of the "Five Whys" is a powerful way businesses and bosses are able to dismantle problems and find creative solutions. The point is that asking why is a useful tool to help us understand life beyond our hearts. It can help us in our jobs, schooling, relationships, and more. However, if we ask why enough, eventually, we will find ourselves back in the territory of the heart.

LAYERS

That great philosopher Shrek was right. There are layers to consider when discussing our inner being. I once had a mentor explain the landscape of the heart with fences. On the outer rim of our hearts, we find a white picket fence that represents selfishness. Selfishness is fairly universal as an outer layer of heart motivation, though not the only possible starting place.

The other day as I was driving, a Scion FR-S cut me off. If you don't know what that car is, it is the yellow one that is most likely to cut you off. I don't know what it is about those cars that makes me think, "I am not sure if that is a sports car or a normal car with an identity crisis," but in my experience, they are the ones most likely to run you off the road. Usually, getting cut off is not a big deal to me, but in this case, after cutting me off, it then rolled through a yellow light in front of me with seemingly expert timing so that I was forced to stop at the red light. Now, I wasn't going anywhere important, and I wasn't running late, but facts like that don't mean very much when the injustice of the situation is so clear. What I mean is, my gut reaction was not a shrug of the shoulders and an assumption that the person who cut me off was an angel on their way to help crippled orphans. . . . In fact, a string of highly creative insults that I am uncomfortable sharing in a public work such as this popped into my mind.

At that moment, I wanted to belittle another person in order to elevate myself. I didn't look it up, but I'm fairly confident the dictionary definition of selfishness involves that motivation. Anytime I put myself as more important than others, selfishness is at work. I use selfishness as the first fence because I would wager that if you are willing to be completely honest with yourself and look back on the last twenty-four hours of your life, you would be able to find an example of selfishness in your own life. In fact, selfish motives are so common that it might be difficult for you to think of one right off the cuff because most people have become accustomed to selfishness; it is hardwired into our everyday lives.

Of course, we are told from culture that selfishness is not a big deal. It is simply baked into our nature because we need selfishness for survival. The "survival of the fittest" philosophy is based entirely on self-preservation and "looking out for number one." The most deceptive line of thinking involves the phrase "Do what makes you happy . . . so long as you aren't hurting anyone." Each of these lines of logic falls apart when they come in contact with Jesus's upside-down kingdom where "those who are last now will be first then, and those who are first will be last" (Matt. 20:16 NLT) and where we are told, "Don't be selfish; don't try to impress others. Be humble, thinking of others as better than yourselves" (Phil. 2:3 NLT). More than this, as we dive deeper into the layers of the heart, we will see how the world's acceptance of selfishness begins to crumble when we see the deeper motives at play.

HONESTY

It is at this point that most people stop. Just like I realize now that I was being selfish when I was unjustly cut off in traffic, it is not difficult to identify your own selfishness. At each stage, when you realize you are in the wrong, make it a regular practice to confess and ask God for forgiveness. Remember that this is not just an exercise in growing as a person, but the goal is to grow as a person in relation to yourself, to others, and to God. Each stage may involve some vulnerable conversations with someone in any of those three categories. Even if you feel like you have hit a breakthrough moment in dealing with selfishness, don't stop there. If you have broken through the white picket fence of selfishness, look up and see that there is another row of fences a little bit closer to the center of your heart. However, I need to issue you a warning. Finding deeper motives is a lot like catching an alligator by the tail: The closer you get to the teeth, the greater the risk.

We will continue to use me as the guinea pig. You may have noticed a hint of how we can move from the outer fence to the next row of fences. We do this by asking good why questions like: *Why* was selfishness there and ready to go at a moment's notice? It is like there was something behind the curtain, shoving my selfish reaction onto the stage and into the spotlight. *Why* would I go to selfishness so quickly? Sit with that question yourself and ask the Lord to reveal the answer to you.

My initial reaction to the injustice came out unchecked. I find it helpful to talk through the events and explain what happened as if I am talking to a friend. (*Spoiler alert!* It's way better to actually talk to a friend!) When I told the story to you, my friend, did you notice that I used a gentle word like "frustration"? In order to move closer to the middle of your heart's motives, look for ways that you soften what you say in order to make yourself look better or more innocent. Everyone becomes an expert in navigating a thesaurus when we try to cover up our inner motives. Frustrated, disappointed, grumpy, and fed up are all just gentle versions of an inner motive called anger.

Of course, there are many examples of explosions of anger that you could identify as the outer fence line of your heart. However, where one of these sins of anger or selfishness exists in my heart, I can usually find the other. The point is that the inner motives of the heart feed the outer motives. It doesn't matter as much which particular sin you find in which location, the one that is hidden is the one that needs your attention and God's forgiveness and healing.

I used to be incredibly competitive. I was a gymnast, which was an individual sport. At one point in middle school, I could not handle doing team sports because I was used to having more control over winning or losing as an individual. If my team was no good, I struggled to enjoy playing because my individual efforts didn't seem to make a difference. There is a finite difference between being competitive and being fueled by anger, even in sports. I saw the person that I was becoming and did not like what I saw. I wanted desperately to enjoy sports again like I did as a kid. I did some digging. I found that anger was lying underneath my symptoms of being competitive to an unhealthy degree, and I confessed to God. Along with that confession, I asked him to help me learn to engage in competition with joy. It took over a year, but God granted me that prayer request.

That is the true power of confession. Too many people imagine a priest and a confessional booth when that word comes up. I recently heard of an unreached people group that came to know the Lord through the work of a missionary my church supported for forty years. When the first convert trusted in Jesus for salvation, she thought she had to remember all her sins and confess them publicly. At the front of the mud hut they called a church building, she numbered her fingers and started confessing; when she ran out of fingers, she moved to her toes. With each digit, she confessed another specific sin, and when she ran out, she looked at our missionary in desperation and said, "There's so much more!"

It would be easy to look at the system I am laying out for diving into your heart and feel like confession is a prescription to get life change. I want to caution you. True confession is less about getting something from God and more about offering yourself to God. True confession is a raw and honest, "God, I need you!" Confession of the surface sins, the outer fence line of your heart, is certainly beneficial, and I would encourage you to include that level of confession in your prayer life, but make sure that you are not just treating the symptoms but pursuing confession of the cause. When you cry out to God to help you because you know that only he can make the change you need to see in your own heart, that is when deep healing and restoration begins.

WHAT ELSE IS ON THE SURFACE?

Before we go any deeper, I wanted to start with selfishness because it is kind of vague but also accessible. Everyone can connect with it immediately. However, there are a lot of fences that we can erect on the outskirts of our hearts. The problem is that most people are so accustomed to their surface-level sin patterns that they can be difficult to identify. In their purest form, the outer levels can be broadly classified as anything we could objectively call a problem, flaw, or sin.

There is always a possibility that a trusted friend will let you down or you will discover that someone you thought was your friend uses you. The pain from abandonment or betrayal can cause some nasty things to grow in your heart. If you find yourself holding a grudge against someone, that is a surface-level issue of your heart. If you see bitterness and pessimism in yourself, those are also signs that deep and destructive roots are feeding those attitudes.

I hope you can see the connection here. The fringe issues of the heart are not hidden but revealed to us by our own outward actions and by our unfiltered stream of thoughts. These are usually the imperfections about ourselves that we are inclined to blame on "the way we are wired" or our "personality." Flaws masquerading as personalities will only feed our insecurities and leave us underdeveloped emotionally, mentally, and spiritually. The regular habit of examining the surface issues and asking why they exist is required for growth.

I also want to mention that while the main focus of this section has been on sin and motives, there is a connection to those dealing with pain or trauma. For those struggling with bitterness, unforgiveness, or self-worth, when you dig past the outer layer of your heart, you may find that those issues were not stemming from a deeper sin but a deeper hurt. The harsh words that still ring in your ear telling you that you are worthless, the physical abuse that you have suppressed to the point of not being able to remember, or even the natural disaster that gives you panic-ridden nightmares, any form of trauma could be lurking beneath the surface-level sin patterns that you see in your heart.

When it comes to these, I want to encourage you to seek the help of someone trusted and emotionally mature enough to handle a conversation about your pain. A pastor, an older and wiser friend, or even a trauma-informed therapist would be incredibly helpful to you. Even though I had an incredibly blessed childhood and my father is my spiritual hero, he is still a human man, and I have had to put in a lot of work on my heart to understand my father wound. Everyone has been hurt by someone close to them, picked up unhealthy habits, or felt the pain of words said in anger or words left unsaid. Do not assume that the pain will have no effect on your heart. Often in an attempt to cover up our trauma or to protect ourselves from future pain, we will develop unhealthy and sinful patterns that manifest themselves as superficial flaws.

Remember that who we are is found in our hearts. When we are hurt on the heart level, it can change us. That should be a sobering reality. No one wants their pain to be in the driver's seat of their life. However, if trauma has made us who we are today, imagine who we will become when Jesus offers us healing in the deepest places of our hearts. That is what it means to live an abundant life. That is the life of freedom that Jesus offers us. Remember, he doesn't just heal your heart, he offers you a new heart.

WHY AGAIN?

If this is the first time that you have been brave enough to dig past the surface levels of your heart and into your hidden motives, you may have experienced some breakthrough moments. However, if you really want to see what God can do with you, you can ask *why* again. Before we go there, I have another warning. After navigating the matters of the heart for decades, I have discovered that the outer fence lines of our hearts are going to be fairly predictable. Moving deeper into our hearts' motives will move us into some uncharted territory. Even if we have worked through our trauma, the tentacles of negative sin patterns can branch out in multiple directions. Asking why can lead us down more than one path. We can't be afraid to journey down multiple paths on our way to the center of our hearts. However, I have found that there is usually one thread to follow that is affecting us deeply.

On this level of the heart, it is all about our identity. Who we are is the center of the target for the enemy. The goal now is to untangle the lies that we believe about ourselves. I will do my best to work through some of the common lies that people believe of themselves, but remember that we have to do the work ourselves to truly see the benefits of reclaiming our identity. We are going beyond the general run-of-the-mill heart responses, and we are crossing a line into specific and personal issues.

For example, in the story of someone cutting me off in traffic, I already have identified selfishness and anger as the fence lines on the outside of my heart. These are common, relatable, and arguably universal responses. However, when I ask myself, "Why am I so quick to indulge my anger?" There could be thousands of potentially correct answers, but only I truly know what motivates that anger.

It could be a trauma response. I could respond in anger because I had my heart broken by a girl in a car, and there is just enough environmental association when I am behind the wheel to trigger a memory of that pain and put me on edge. I could be disappointed and discouraged by unmet expectations. I could be quietly brooding over feelings of unfulfillment in my career, stuffing down my emotions, and this event is simply the last straw. It could be a feeling of inadequacy. I could be struggling with feeling pulled between my schedule and my responsibilities as a husband and father. It could even be delusions of grandeur. The source of the anger could be that I truly believe that I am untouchable and better than others and that everything is everyone else's fault.

Let's look back at that list: trauma, disappointment, inadequacy, delusions of grandeur. Let us add to that a desperate need for security, feeling like we are a burden to others, restlessness, dissatisfaction, relational instability, and the list goes on. The point is that this level of heart identity is where we will find that the lines between mental health, emotional health, and spiritual health begin to blur. This is also why understanding and believing who we are in Christ is so important.

> But you are not like that, for you are a chosen people. You are royal priests, a holy nation, God's very own possession. As a result, you can show others the goodness of God, for he called you out of the darkness into his wonderful light.
>
> "Once you had no identity as a people;
> now you are God's people.
> Once you received no mercy;
> now you have received God's mercy."
> (1 Pet. 2:9–10 NLT)

We are God's people. It is the greatest life hack of all time. It is incredibly important for us to learn the skills of knowing who we are on the inside and how that changes the entirety of our being, but if we want a massive shortcut, just focus on identifying as belonging to God. Each of the difficult and tragic issues that lie in this tier of our hearts shares the same goal: to try to convince us that we are something we are not. We combat issues of identity in our hearts by dismantling the lies we believe about ourselves.

How do you know if you are lying to yourself? Well, there are a number of good ways to find out what lies you believe. The first way is to study what the Bible has to say about you. That is a lot of what I have written about so far in this book. My goal has been to show you biblically who you are created to be and give you the skills you need to continue to pursue that identity. Most Christians I know are obsessed with knowing what God has called them to *do*, but I want you to be obsessed with who he has called you to *be*.

The second way to dismantle the lies you believe about yourself is to let someone actually know you. The greatest spiritual turning point for me in my life besides getting saved was the day that I fully committed to be honest with my accountability group, the Warriors, at my church. It is a rarity in the human experience to have no secrets from someone. Most people cannot imagine what it is like to pursue this kind of friendship outside of marriage, and many people cannot even comprehend a marriage with this much transparency. However, anyone who has been brave enough to have a rich relationship with a trusted and spiritually mature friend of the same gender will tell you that you need someone who will help you identify your blind spots.

WHAT'S THE POINT?

If we attempt to change our behaviors—those pesky things in our lives that don't make us act like Jesus—without changing our motives, our successes will be short-lived and futile. It is only by examining and changing our motives that we can make long-term changes to our outer actions. Our motives and impulses are also information we can use to discover more about ourselves.

The inner levels of our hearts that lie beneath our motives hold our identity. What we believe about who we are informs our motives and, ultimately, our actions. Some people go so far as to use this inner level of their heart to hack their lives. They wake up in the morning and ask themselves, "If I were a person who works out, what would I do when my alarm goes off?" Convincing themselves that they are a particular kind of person is a strong way to change motives and, therefore, actions. It connects identity to desire. In our case, rather than preaching affirmations to ourselves in the mirror, we need to believe what God believes about who we are and allow him to change our lives.

Father, be merciful to me. You have been so patient and kind as I have stumbled through this journey of learning to understand my heart and who you created me to be. Grant me the courage to continue on the journey and establish myself as a person who knows why I do what I do. Help me. Change my desires and motives that lie underneath the surface of my actions and make me more like Jesus.

Amen

CHAPTER SEVEN

I DON'T BELIEVE YOU

I stood outside his office with conflicting emotions. I knew that once I opened that door, there was nowhere to hide. I knew that I would answer every question as honestly as I could, and yet, there seemed to be a point at which I would always be stuck. I took a deep breath and opened the door. Every time I stood in the threshold of that office space, I felt a resistance. However, every time I was actually in the office talking with my youth pastor and my friends, being brutally honest felt natural. I took my seat, engaged in a few minutes of small talk, and then the question came: "Jason, how was your heart this week?" *Deep breath . . .*

It is always easier to start with the fence line furthest from the center of the heart, so I answered, "Well, I really didn't even think about picking up my Bible this week. I just got busy." Everyone listened with understanding, but we all knew there was more.

"Everyone is busy, why do you think this week it has been more of a challenge?" Tab, my youth leader, asked.

I responded, "I know, I am just frustrated with school. It feels like all they want from me is busywork. I want to do something that matters."

The questions kept coming. "Why do you think you feel like God can't use you at school?" Or "Why do you feel like it is easier to blame school when this is an issue between you and God?" Or "Why do you think God has you at that school?" Or "Why do you think your frustrations end with you not wanting to read the Bible?"

I began to feel like there wasn't much of a point to these meetings if every honest answer I gave ended with being asked another *why* question. Stubbornly, I sat week after week on the beanbags in Tab's office, trying to find a satisfying answer to the question why. I would have thought that I was the only one with this problem if it wasn't for a few good friends who kept showing up week after week with me. After years of moving from the shallows to the deep parts of my heart with this group, I finally broke through to the central problem.

In the journey to the center of my heart, I found it to be much like a spider's web. Some probing questions led me closer to the center of my heart like the concentric rings that form the iconic target shape of a spider web, while other questions led me in a lateral direction. Often, the interlacing of each part of my heart connected pieces of myself that I did not think were related. By the time we finally arrived at the center of my heart, I had a very clear sense of its structure. In its complexity, I discovered a lot of hidden motives behind my actions. I also felt that I understood myself.

You do not want to approach your own journey to the center of your heart in one simple line. You need the journey if you want to truly know yourself. Do not shy away from the rabbit trails and seemingly unrelated issues of your heart in a rush to find the center. In the center of your heart, you will find a battle that rages for your soul, but it is not complicated. The questions you want answered about yourself are found not at the center of your heart but right on the edge of the center. Do not rush past the process.

Honestly, I don't remember the exact line of questions that led me, with Tab's help, to the center of my heart, but I do remember how it felt. When I was young, my dad told me that people who harvested pearls had a technique for holding their breath for a long time. Sitting on the edge of the pool, he showed me how to breathe deeply through my nose and slowly out of my mouth. He showed me how to control intentional hyperventilation safely and to calm myself in the water. With slow, deliberate movements, we could stay under the water for close to a minute with our overly oxygenated blood. Eventually, the urge to breathe overwhelmed my desire to stay at the bottom of the deep end, and rising to the surface, I would take a deep and refreshing breath. Finding the center of my heart felt like that. I was comfortable at the bottom of the pool, but as I reached the surface, the urge to breathe became the most important thing in the world.

I will tell you what is at the center of your heart, but I need you to understand something about the nature of your heart. As we have journeyed closer to the center of your heart, it has been like holding on to a rope that is tied to an anchor. You know what is at the surface, but the pressure gets intense as you follow the rope deeper into the water. Ultimately, you know what is at the end of the rope. It is an anchor. This anchor represents your belief. The question shifts from "What is at the end of the rope?" to "How is the anchor secured?" Where the anchor rests has the greatest impact on everything that is attached to it. It is not if you believe but what you believe that is important.

Our hearts' biggest problem is unbelief—specifically when we choose to believe lies about who God is and our relationship with him. There are so many subtle ways we choose every day not to believe something about God or about who we are to God. I know that this might feel overly simple, especially because of the complexity of the web, which is the map of your heart. However, simple truths are often the ones that, when understood and applied, yield the greatest results. Your beliefs are an anchor for your heart. Now the question is: What is true that you choose not to believe? Most of the time, our unbelief is not believing that God is who he says he is.

WHERE IS THE UNBELIEF?

Tab asked a lot of good *why* questions to help me figure out that there was a core truth of who God is that I was subtly refusing to believe and that disbelief was fueling all my insecurities about relationships in my life. If I was consumed by what other people thought of me, what did I struggle to believe about God? First of all, I didn't believe that he liked me. It is easy to read John 3:16 and talk about God's love in the context of global love. It is easy to look at what Jesus suffered on the cross as a requirement to appease God's wrath. It was even easy for me to personally believe that he would save me from my sin because of Jesus's substitutionary atonement. The point is, this particular root of unbelief was present even when I had saving faith and belief in Jesus. However, there was still a sliver of my heart that felt like God's favor was something I needed to earn. Subconsciously, I wanted to offer him something that only I could give him. More than that, if I did the right things, God would be obligated to bless me according to the ways that I wanted him to bless me.

Which also shows that I was struggling to believe that God has good plans for me.

The crazy thing is that I knew God loves me personally and has plans for me; but somewhere deep in my heart, I needed to fight the lie that he didn't. It is so difficult to communicate the potential influence these revelations can have on your life. The beautiful thing about this part of your spiritual journey is that God has a plan for you specifically. That plan includes increasing your faith in all areas. For me, inviting a few trusted brothers to speak into my life sped up the process. I have so many friends who are on this journey now but have had to carve their own path. The right people asking the right questions at the right time can be used powerfully by God to make the most of these breakthrough moments. However, the actual, practical application of this whole chapter rests firmly on your shoulders. The question you ask yourself must shift from "Why do I do what I do?" to "What do I struggle to believe?"

I want to make this crystal clear. This is not a book about the theology of belief. However, it is helpful to touch on a bit of a theological issue at this point to help clarify what we are talking about. I don't want you to be afraid that you are at risk of losing your salvation just because you have doubts or areas of your heart that have believed a lie. It is possible to have saving faith in Jesus and still fight to believe 100 percent of the good news that comes with that faith. The comfort that you and I can take from Jesus's own lips is that after we come to faith in Christ, our eternal destination is ultimately no longer our responsibility. Look at this passage about the role of belief and what Jesus does on behalf of those who believe.

> Jesus replied, "I have already told you, and you don't believe me. The proof is the work I do in my Father's

> name. But you don't believe me because you are not my sheep. My sheep listen to my voice; I know them, and they follow me. I give them eternal life, and they will never perish. No one can snatch them away from me, for my Father has given them to me, and he is more powerful than anyone else. No one can snatch them from the Father's hand. The Father and I are one."
>
> Once again the people picked up stones to kill him. (John 10:25–31 NLT)

Jesus is serious about your eternal security. If you are one of his sheep, he is willing to risk his life, not only to save you but to make sure you know that he will keep you. There are only a handful of times that Jesus overtly links himself to God the Father to the point that people are willing to kill him. During this time, if someone claimed to be God, that was called blaspheming and was punishable by death. The people knew that he was backing up his ability to forgive sins, grant us a place in eternity, and secure that place in eternity. Only God can do that. It is no mistake that he connects his authority to establish eternal security to his Trinitarian relationship with the Father.

Even this issue of eternal security is affected by a lingering seed of unbelief in the hearts of humanity. If your testimony is anything like mine, you have been a Christian for years. In fact, I prayed the sinner's prayer at the age of five. Now, with time passing, and especially since I have seen the immaturity of my own kids at the age of five, it makes me wonder if I really understood enough to have saving faith at that age. However, faith like a child is not bogged down by theology. Faith like a child doesn't feel that it has to defend itself. Faith like a child simply believes. That is the thing about the gospel; it is simple. I am guilty, and Jesus took my punishment so that I could be right with God. Of course, there is a lot more! The Holy Spirit, adoption as sons, being part of the bride of Christ, the process of sanctification, and the list goes on. This leaves so much room in our lives for questions, doubts, long-term growth, and even seasons of unbelief. Jesus is still able to hold us in his hand.

PETER'S FAITH

Matthew 16 is an excellent example of this in action. You should take the time to read the whole chapter slowly and really meditate on it, but for now, I will give you an overview. The chapter begins with the religious leaders pestering Jesus to perform a miracle. He does not, confuses them with a brilliant story from the Old Testament, and leaves. Then he warns his disciples about these manipulative religious leaders, and they are confused because they are "hangry." Jesus calls them out, surprised at their lack of faith. Finally, the lightbulb begins to show signs of life as they recognize that there are more important things than food.

The next thing that happens is like a scene change in a stage play. The story picks up again in another city. I like to imagine that Peter is uncharacteristically quiet while he walks the dirt road behind Jesus. He is not only pondering what has just happened but truly weighing the claims Jesus has made, what he knows of this man, and who he believes Jesus is. Jesus lets him think. He gives him plenty of time to come to his own conclusion. He waits until they have arrived at their destination and are all settled from their travels before he asks his big question.

> "Who do people say that the Son of Man is?"
>
> "Well," they replied, "some say John the Baptist, some say Elijah, and others say Jeremiah or one of the other prophets."

> Then he asked them, "But who do you say I am?"
> Simon Peter answered, "You are the Messiah, the Son of the living God." (Matt. 16:13–16 NLT)

When Peter replies, he gets it right! He knows that Jesus is not only the Savior promised to the nation of Israel, but that he is also God's Son. Jesus affirms his faith, gives Peter a new name, and commissions him to be the head of the church. Everything is going great for Peter! We can clearly see how his faith and belief have grown since the previous passage. That is, until Jesus starts talking again.

While Peter's faith is at its peak, Jesus begins to speak openly about what is going to happen next. He is going to die, be buried for three days, and come back to life. This was not how Peter imagined the Son of God would save the world. In fact, he couldn't wrap his mind around how dying would help anyone!

> Peter took him aside and began to reprimand him for saying such things. "Heaven forbid, Lord," he said. "This will never happen to you!"
> Jesus turned to Peter and said, "Get away from me, Satan! You are a dangerous trap to me. You are seeing things merely from a human point of view, not from God's." (Matt. 16:22–23 NLT)

I think we can all sympathize with Peter. Just when life seems to be making sense, God throws a curveball. He was on the right track, saying the right things, even believing the right things, but as soon as Jesus went past his understanding, his faith was shaken. I know exactly what that feels like. My desire to understand or even know a sliver of the future has a massive effect on my ability to exercise my faith. The practical exercise of faith makes me uncomfortable, but that doesn't mean it's wrong.

BELIEF

God is not concerned with your ability to understand him. He is concerned with your willingness to believe him. That is why Jesus taught the way that he taught. There are a lot of examples of people asking Jesus questions in the New Testament, and he rarely gave a direct answer. It was not uncommon for Jesus to respond to questions with more questions. Sometimes a direct answer is not as beneficial to receive as an invitation to follow Jesus deeper into the heart of the issue.

It is often said that Jesus spoke to the heart. This is not only because of the messages he delivered but because he kept asking questions. He skillfully guides us to find the answers ourselves because that is how we learn deep truths most effectively. I was so relieved when my two-year-old daughter got a very minor burn on her hand after touching a hot pot while my wife cooked. We warned her it was hot, told her not to touch it, and kept her from touching it, but she found a way to touch it anyway when no one was looking. Praise the Lord it was minor, and praise the Lord that it happened! There is only so much instruction can teach us. Sometimes, the only way we will learn is from touching the hot thing and finding out for ourselves that what we heard is true. The deeper the truth, the more beneficial it becomes for us to discover it for ourselves. Jesus understands this principle so he will lead you with questions.

By now, we know that asking why ultimately leads us to the place in our hearts where we struggle with unbelief. This was intentional in Jesus's strategy. As we continue to study Scripture, we will begin to see this theme jumping out at us from every angle. Jesus talks a lot about faith, belief, and the nature of the kingdom of God, and he asks questions. Jesus's impact is ongoing today because he knew that communicating to us through our hearts would go beyond ancient Israel, beyond the modern era, and last for eternity. The Word of God is eternally beneficial because it is directed at the heart.

The heart is valuable. We have talked about that value in terms of our emotional health, mental health, and spiritual health, but it is ultimately valuable because what we believe is what is in our hearts. In fact, I would go so far as to say that it is cosmically valuable. Consider this: When Satan tempted Jesus in the wilderness, his first strategy was to appeal to Jesus's physical discomfort. He wanted Jesus to perform a miracle for nothing more than personal comfort. He wanted Jesus to do something entirely self-serving, and it wouldn't hurt anyone. If Jesus were to succumb to this temptation, it would be out of a selfish motive with a root of unbelief that God was able to provide and sustain him. That is why he answered that the Word of God was food enough for him (see Matt. 4:4).

The second attack came when Jesus was transported to the top of the temple. Satan was appealing to Jesus's sense of personal safety while also offering him the world. This one is interesting because Satan quoted Scripture, trying to get Jesus to doubt God's own words. Jesus had to decide if he believed the Word of the Father to the point that he did not need proof.

> Next the devil took him to the peak of a very high mountain and showed him all the kingdoms of the world and their glory. "I will give it all to you," he said, "if you will kneel down and worship me."
>
> "Get out of here, Satan," Jesus told him. "For the Scriptures say,

> 'You must worship the LORD your God
> and serve only him.'" (Matt. 4:8–10 NLT)

This third interaction shows us what is really going on behind the scenes. The indirect route the devil takes to attempt to sow seeds of doubt in Jesus's heart did not work. Finally, we see the direct confrontation and what Satan is really after. The thing that he really wants is for Jesus to kneel and worship him. This is a loaded request. The act of kneeling is a sign of humbling yourself before someone else. It universally communicates that you see yourself as lower than the other. The act of worship is an act of faith. The devil doesn't just want Jesus humbled before him; he wants outward evidence of an inward belief that he is really deserving of power, love, and honor. This request from Satan to Jesus is so audacious that it hurts my mind to even consider it.

The brazen nature of this request is good for us to see in Scripture. I can only imagine that the devil made such a request with no twist, no deception, and no strategy because he was desperate and frustrated. This interaction truly shows us how unmatched the enemy is against Jesus. It also shows us exactly what the enemy wants from us. Ultimately, Satan wants our faith, our belief, to shift away from God and to him. If he knows that there is no hope and we will not give it to him, he will do everything he can to attack the foundation of our belief. It is far better for him if we believe nothing. It is a big loss for him if we experience doubt but do the hard work and trust Jesus again. When we know the enemy's motivation behind attacks aimed at our faith, dismantling them becomes so much easier.

Why did the enemy want proof of faith? Why did the devil want Jesus to believe in him? In our humanity, and as we talk about belief, it is easy to view the one who needs the faith of others as weak. For example, I imagine a father leaning in to whisper in his daughter's ear before the final track meet of the season, saying, "Whatever happens, I believe in you." In that moment, the father is the one who is showing strength, and the daughter needs to know that Dad is in her corner. Dad is strong, offering strength to his daughter who needs that internal strength. However, belief doesn't work like that with God. He is not the daughter, seeking the approval of a higher strength.

He is the strong one in our relationship, so belief in this cosmically big power looks different. Belief is not like a cake that we are holding in our hands, free to offer to anyone we like. Belief in God is more like potential. At least, that is how Jesus talks about it. There is far more than you could think or imagine that God wants to do in us (Eph. 3:16–21). Faith in our hearts is how God fuels that potential. So, while belief is cosmically valuable to God, it is not because of what we offer him. It is because of what he can do through us.

Think of it this way: The most drastic change in your life happened because of belief. The moment that your head and your heart connected and the beauty of the gospel came through your ears and resonated in your heart and you believed it, you were transferred from the kingdom of darkness into the kingdom of light. You went from being on the bad guy's team to being on the good guy's team. Your name is on the roster, but are you going to put on the jersey? Are you going to travel with the team? Are you going to find a spot to park your keister in the stands? Will you run onto the field and commit your life to being a star player? Are you even ready to be on the field, or do you need to heal first? That is what happened to Paul. He spent three years being discipled after his conversion before he began his missionary ministry. The whole time, God's plan was to use him to be a key figure in the advancement of his kingdom.

Don't fall into the trap that the purer your belief, the more drastic your calling will be. However, the bigger your faith, the more willing you will find yourself to chase after the things that make God smile. That may mean that your life will take drastic turns and land you in situations that don't sound like a lot of fun to the rest of the world. The point is that increasing your belief and ridding yourself of places where you choose to doubt God's character will transform your life. As a bonus, you will find that you love the life he has prepared for you most of all.

DANGEROUS PRAYERS

It is no small thing to focus your attention and time on growing your faith in God. As you can imagine, the closer you get to the center of your heart, the more resistance you will face from the enemy. Believe me when I tell you that the payoff is worth it because God offers you more of himself. If you don't know where to begin, my recommendation is to pray a dangerous prayer.

You are likely familiar with a few dangerous prayers. For example, if we ask God to grant us patience, it is likely that he will begin to put us in situations where we are forced to practice that patience. In the same way, there are two prayers that come with the territory of belief that are also dangerous.

The first is simply to ask him to increase our faith. This seems harmless enough, but we will likely find ourselves in positions where we must exercise our faith. The problem with exercising faith is that it can only happen when we can't see a way out. What I mean is that faith is unseen. This means that life may throw us curveballs, and we will have to prepare ourselves to practice faith, practice choosing to believe even when we don't feel a way out. This may be in a tense relationship, an argument with an atheist, or even in the midst of an internal battle. The landscape for this struggle will vary, so prepare well with prayer and invite God into your circumstances as regularly as possible.

The second dangerous prayer is to ask God to show us any place in our hearts where we struggle with unbelief. This prayer is intense, and it will take us into some deep places of our hearts. Be prepared because God may begin the process of leading us to unbelief by exposing sin in our lives. I have already written extensively on taking this particular tiger by the tail and working our way to the real issue lying beneath.

I had a dear friend named Charles Stucky who went to be with Jesus a number of years ago. One of the things he said was that "God is so beyond what we can comprehend that we will ever be learning more about him, even in glory." This has always stuck in my mind. It was the first time in my life that I considered that God was beyond what I would be physically able to understand. I mention this because if God is so much bigger than we think he is, there will always be more opportunities to expand our belief in him. Please don't let this reality discourage you but encourage you. It is an opportunity to find him more entertaining, more valuable, more captivating, more gracious, more merciful, more kind, more just, and so on than we would consider possible in one being. There is ever more to discover about him, and the more we uncover, the more opportunities we will have to grow in our faith.

God, I echo the prayer of the desperate man who said, "I believe, help my unbelief!" I want to see my faith in you grow. I want the confidence that comes with knowing who you are, knowing who I am, and knowing that I can trust you in every area of my heart. I want to pray the dangerous prayers. Show me what I struggle to believe about you. Show me where I am not in alignment with who you made me to be. Give me a heart that feels what you feel and prioritizes what you prioritize. Help me take my commitment to you to the next level and grow my faith in who you are. Remind me that you walk closely with me and I am never alone.

Amen

SECTION THREE

CHAPTER EIGHT

THE ART OF VULNERABILITY

Secrets, secrets are no fun.
Secrets, secrets hurt someone.

Napoleon knew he should be surveying the battlefield. The conditions were perfect. The early morning mist cleared over Waterloo as the sun made its slow ascent. The plan was always to begin just before the light of day and give the enemy no opportunity to see his troops' positions, but there was a problem. Hemorrhoids were the problem. Author and historian Phil Mason blames the fall of Napoleon's army at the Battle of Waterloo on his ongoing struggle with hemorrhoids.[1]

Apparently, all signs point to Napoleon's original plan of an early morning attack being delayed because he was unable to mount his horse and survey the battlefield. As a result, it was nearing midday before the battle began, allowing the opposing forces to make key adjustments and prepare for battle. It is a real possibility that if Napoleon had been able to mount his horse, begin his attack, and move his troops according to his strategic genius, he could have won the battle.

It wasn't until Napoleon's brother Jerome was close to death that he confessed he was one of only three people who knew about his brother's hemorrhoids that day. Napoleon was intentionally shrouded in mystery, especially any details of his life that would make him seem like a normal, mortal man. To a certain degree, it worked. It is hard to argue with the results, and the infamous name, Napoleon, is a household name to this day. However, if even a handful of his most trusted generals had been allowed to know what was really going on behind the scenes with their leader, they might have survived that day.

While I certainly hope you are not suffering from hemorrhoids, I also hope that you are not going through life in radical secrecy like Napoleon. Napoleon and those three people closest to him suffered from the assumption that appearing invulnerable is a sign of strength. Worse still, it cost the lives of twenty-five thousand men who perished on the battlefield.

Dr. Brené Brown has written extensively on the benefits of vulnerability. She writes, "Vulnerability is not winning or losing; it's having the courage to show up and be seen when we have no control over the outcome. Vulnerability is not weakness; it's our greatest measure of courage."[2] Therefore, Napoleon's lack of vulnerability was cowardice, not on the battlefield, but in relationships with others. The history of the world could have been seriously altered if he had the courage to be vulnerable and ask for help.

How did you feel when you read the word *vulnerability* in the chapter title? My gut reaction to this word is to prickle up and try to roll away like a hedgehog. It feels uncomfortable. It feels exposed. It feels dangerous. It feels that way because it *is* uncomfortable, exposing, and dangerous. It is also liberating, life-giving, relationship-building, the first step toward healing, and the only way to have a genuine identity. The benefits far outweigh the risks.

You should know by now, dear reader, that matters of the heart are often found in the tension between personal risk and life-giving benefit. So how do we push past the risky parts of being vulnerable with our hearts and tap into the healing benefits of having a vulnerable heart? The first step is the most important. We must first be vulnerable to God. Only then will we be able to be vulnerable with people.

You may fear vulnerability because you have tried it with people before being vulnerable with God. It isn't likely that vulnerability can be healthy when we do it in reverse like this because vulnerability becomes poisoned by insecurity. Insecurity makes us always look for ways to hide who or what we are. We want to hide the tender or broken places of our hearts from pain. However, deep pain in our hearts begins to define our identity. That is the birthplace of insecurity. Insecurity is a false identity growing inside our hearts that we can defeat when we turn our hearts over to God in vulnerability.

How does this look in relationships? How about that friend who uses "prayer requests" as a way to gossip about others? Or the friend who is incredibly nice but refuses to have deep conversations. Worst of all are people who identify their own problems, pain, or sin but blame them on their personality. This is false vulnerability. Humility is an admired trait in the church, and many people confuse this with talking down about themselves. This is confession without repentance. We are called to pursue a renewed heart, and only God can do the restoration. That is why the key to life-giving vulnerability is to be radically vulnerable toward God before attempting to be vulnerable with God's people.

Because he knows everything about us, being truly vulnerable with him is not a risk in the same way that vulnerability toward people can be. Through the process of exposing our hearts to him, he also reveals more of who we really are in Christ. So if you want to know who you are, expose your heart to its creator. That means he must know everything about you because he created everything and knows everything about everything. That's a lot of everythings.

It is so easy to know about this concept in our minds and ignore the implications of his sovereignty on our hearts. Don't fall into the trap of assuming you can hide yourself from him. If you do, you will apply all of the dangers involved with being vulnerable with people to God. We may notice we have been doing this without knowing when we find ourselves thinking, "What if they get to know me and they don't like me?" or "What would people say if they knew what I was thinking?" or "How could someone love me if they knew what I have done?"

If we believe that the Bible is true, we know that all these concerns are washed away by the blood of Jesus for those who believe. Psalm 139:14 says that you are "fearfully and wonderfully made." First Peter 2:9 says, "You are a chosen race, a royal priesthood, a holy nation, a people for his own possession." First John 3:1 says, "See what kind of love the Father has given to us, that we should be called children of God." I reference all these verses to show that God not only knows us but he decided from the moment he had his knitting needles out that he *likes* us. There is nothing within us that will surprise him, yet, for some reason, we keep trying to hide our hearts from him.

Even now, you likely have something in your heart that you would rather not discuss with God. You know in your mind that he must know about it, but maybe if you are able to ignore it, he will do the same. It is to those places that we must go in order to mine vulnerability for its benefits. It is to those places where we feel our hearts begin to resist that we must press in for a deeper relationship with God. He wants us to draw near to him, to pursue him. He wants us to find out firsthand about the depths of his love and goodness that feel like uncharted territory to us. He wants to speak healing into the tender places of our hearts that feel broken beyond repair. Most of all, he wants to remove our insecurities.

Insecurities are false identities growing inside our hearts. God wants to guide us, through vulnerability with him, to those false identities so we can watch as he tears them down by calling us his children, royal priests, his creation made in his image. The benefit of vulnerability toward God is the discovery of restored identity in the place where our insecurities die.

As we dive deeper into our hearts by being vulnerable toward God, I would like you to do something. Pray out loud. It is so easy to pray in our heads, but the impact of words spoken out loud is stronger for some reason. There is nothing magical or extra spiritual about praying out loud, but it is one small thing we can do to actively show God and ourselves that we are willing to be vulnerable. In fact, take a moment right now and pray aloud to him.

* * *

How did that feel? Was it uncomfortable? It is okay to feel uncomfortable. Praying aloud never starts out feeling right to me. In fact, I will pray for a minute, look around to make sure no one is watching me, and then go right back to it. It's almost like I am afraid that someone will be standing in the doorway ready to video me. Does it feel strange? Are you afraid to get caught praying? It sounds funny, but so many of us struggle with these fears! That strange feeling is a big part of vulnerability. Just because it is strange, don't allow it to make you hide.

WE WERE NOT MADE TO HIDE

"Then the eyes of both were opened, and *they knew* that they were naked. And *they sewed* fig leaves together and made themselves loincloths. And *they heard* the sound of the LORD God walking in the garden in the cool of the day, and *the man and his wife hid* themselves from the presence of the LORD God among the trees of the garden."

Genesis 3:7–8—emphasis mine

Think about Adam and Eve. They were the first people to choose to attempt to hide themselves and their hearts from God. Instead of choosing to be honest and vulnerable with God, they ran away. Let me set the scene: The worst thing to ever happen in the history of humankind has happened. Adam and Eve chose to rebel against the easiest rule given to them by the creator of the universe: "Don't eat that."

Of course, just like telling a kid, "Whatever you do, don't push that giant red button," Adam and Eve do the thing they are not supposed to do. They believe the lies of the serpent and eat from the Tree of the Knowledge of Good and Evil. There are entire books written about this event and all that follows, but consider what happens next. Specifically, pay attention to the actions Adam and Eve take to keep from being vulnerable to God. These are the moments that follow their first taste of rebellion:

They knew, they sewed, they heard, and they hid. If we apply a little bit of transparent motivation to these actions, we get this:

1. They knew the problem
2. They covered up the problem
3. They heard God call
4. They hid from God

I have four kids, so I am very familiar with this pattern. If they are in trouble, they know what they did, try to cover it up, feel fear in my presence, and hide. You should be able to recognize this same pattern in your life. How do I know? I know that it is within all of humankind to act in this way because the same sinful nature of Adam lived in every one of us at some point of our lives. We don't like to be vulnerable—it's not in our DNA.

Do not treat this behavior lightly, however comfortable you or the people in your life have become with this progression. This pattern of sin and pain is incredibly destructive to relationships. It's almost like it is designed to sink its hooks into a healthy relationship and rip it apart. In fact, that is exactly what happened to Adam and Eve in their relationship with God! The sin breeds distrust, cowardice, lying, argument, bitterness, and a host of other painful side effects.

Vulnerability is the willingness to expose or discover the inner parts of our hearts. This means that in order to be vulnerable, we must be able to discover the real us and then be willing to share with someone else. We can be vulnerable with ourselves, with other people, and particularly with God. This is why the temptation to hide is so strong. Not only does radical vulnerability push us to uncomfortable conversations with other people but also to potentially uncomfortable conversations with ourselves.

It is not until we take a step back and look at the long-term and destructive effects of hiding from others that we can pursue vulnerable relationships. Hiding our true selves will always tear apart relationships, not build them. Vulnerability leads to relational growth and freedom. What we find in Adam and Eve's story is that their relationship with God, which was originally pure and vulnerable, fell apart quickly because of their fear of being found out. It makes me wonder how God would have reacted to Adam and Eve if instead of running away, they ran to him.

Let's examine the four actions Adam and Eve took that led them to make the decision to hide from God. In each case, a willingness to be radically vulnerable with God with our broken heart drastically changes the dynamic of our relationship with him. It is important to note before we examine Adam and Eve's four actions that this exercise works for all areas of brokenness. The beautiful thing about God's grace is that it is not limited to work only on sin. His grace can also heal the areas of our hearts that have been decimated by the *effects* of sin.

What I mean is this: God doesn't just want us to be vulnerable with our hearts so that we become excellent at sin management. He wants to apply his tender love, grace, mercy, and healing to all the places in our hearts that have been injured or damaged by others as well. For example, we may have been verbally abused. Radical vulnerability toward God is a massive part of the healing process. We were not at fault by receiving verbal abuse, but we can absolutely still go down the path of shame and hiding from God. It will even show itself in the same four steps that Adam and Eve took to run from God:

We know the problem. The lies and anger that another person spewed on us through verbal abuse hurt us deeply. There is a place in our heart that is injured and in need of comfort and restoration. However, we fear that if we admit to the pain, we surrender ourselves to being under the authority of the person who hurt us.

We cover up the problem. Because we don't want our abuser or anyone else to know that their words hit our hearts like a dagger, rather than remove the dagger and deal with the mess, we tell ourselves, others, and God an all-too-common lie, "I'm fine."

We hear God's call. It could be a church service, a small group conversation, a moment in private devotion, an Instagram post, or a random thought that hits us while we are sitting at a red light. At some point, God calls us, bringing the moment to mind, and we have to make a choice.

We hide. If we are honest, we usually don't do the right thing the first time. When backed into a corner, we shut down and stay quiet rather than expose the truth. Eventually, though we knew the abusive words spoken over us were a lie, we began to act as if they were true and took on a false identity informed by our trauma. A lie hidden long enough will erode our character and turn us into the very thing we fear to become.

This is not a pleasant outcome, but I want us to see the pattern emerging. It is important to know the risks associated with hiding from God. We will now see Adam and Eve go through these same steps. We will learn how to identify this pattern so that we will never slip into it unintentionally again. Even if we feel like our lives have been defined by this pattern, God offers healing and hope if we are willing to grow in vulnerability. In each of the four actions Adam and Eve took, look for the ways vulnerability could have changed their hearts.

NUMBER 1—THEY KNEW

"Then the eyes of both were opened,
and they knew that they were naked."

Genesis 3:7

Adam and Eve's eyes were opened when they sinned. We always act like the tree was a giant problem for the first couple. I doubt it really matters what kind of tree it was. Apple, orange, or kumquat isn't the point of the story. The point of the story is found in the name of the tree: the Tree of the *Knowledge* of Good and Evil. The serpent knew this "secret knowledge" was what made the fruit look sweet. Remember what he said to Eve? "God knows that when you eat of it your eyes will be opened, and you will be like God, *knowing* good and evil" (Gen. 3:5—emphasis mine).

That part of the snake's lie was true. And they got the knowledge. However, anyone who has struggled with a pornography addiction will tell you that having knowledge of things that were intended to remain hidden is not worth the guilt and shame attached to that knowledge. Satan's lie was in the implication that this knowledge of good and evil did not come with a cost. Adam and Eve were the first to learn this lesson the hard way. They knew in a moment that they could not unring the bell of their disobedience. Regret and shame now entered the world and their lives forever.

Imagine how vulnerability would have changed the story if applied after Adam and Eve's "eyes [were] opened." What if instead of following the path of sin and shame, they chose to be open about their mistake? They would have had to be willing to speak the words that very few people are humble enough to say to another person: *I need you.*

"I need you" feels weak. "I can do it myself" feels empowering. Admitting our need for others is a skill to be developed. This stubbornness we all share that won't allow us to admit our need to others transcends gender, age, ethnicity, and upbringing. We all have pride that stands in the way of our ability to admit that we need help. In most cases, people will even go so far as to try manipulation rather than admit to their core needs.

However, this drive to protect our image forces us to put up an appearance of being strong. Nothing could be further from the truth. We must be willing to admit to ourselves and to God, "I need you."

As soon as we know, God knows too. There is no need to try to cover up with a flashy but empty attempt at a show of strength. A better option is to start with honesty. Trust me, there is nothing we can do that will shock him. He has known about this moment from the beginning of time. He longs for us to cry out to him *before* he calls out, "Where are you?" As soon as we know, we can choose to make our hearts vulnerable to the Lord. We will find that he responds with comfort, grace, and the sweetness of his presence.

NUMBER 2—THEY SEWED FIG LEAVES TOGETHER (COVERED UP)

"And they sewed fig leaves together and
made themselves loincloths."

Genesis 3:7

Fig trees are an important symbol in Scripture. I never appreciated them until I had one. It was awful. First of all, they attract wasps because the female wasp pollinates the tree by burrowing herself in juvenile figs, dying, and then being "absorbed" (I prefer *eaten*) by the tree. That's right, the fig tree eats wasps. Every time you eat a fig, you are eating fully digested wasp juice . . . yum.

This isn't even the most fascinating thing about fig trees! The best part of the fig trees is the leaves. I can see why Adam and Eve wanted these leaves because they are just the right size to cover strategic areas of the human physique . . . if you get my drift. However, I can attest from experience that they are also irritating to the skin. Not as irritating as poison ivy, but certainly not comfortable to wear around one's nether regions. The leaves feel a bit like velvet and Velcro fell in love and had an uncomfortable baby.

I have a serious theory that the detail of fig leaves in this story is intentional. I believe God wanted us to know that when we try to cover up our sin, it's going to be uncomfortable. Remember the days of your innocence when you felt your stomach rise up to your throat when you knew you were in trouble? It is natural to feel uncomfortable when you are in the presence of sin. This is called guilt, and it can be a good thing. We don't like guilt for a number of reasons. First, guilt means that we are wrong. Second, it doesn't feel good. Third, guilt is usually followed by punishment. Fourth and worst of all, guilt likes to hold hands with shame.

Here is how guilt is a good thing: It is part of the internal warning system that tells us something is wrong. When that warning goes off, it is time to come clean. Guilt is a good thing that keeps us from stealing. Money, someone's car, or someone's wife would all be fair game, and there would be no emotional motivation to keep our whole society from spiraling into self-destruction. Guilt keeps us socially in line. Guilt also has spiritual benefits. We know that guilt is what drives us to know that we need Jesus. Paul says it best: "If it had not been for the law, I would not have known sin" (Rom. 7:7).

The purpose of the law was to show us that we are guilty apart from Christ. It's so important to cling to God's grace and become vulnerable with him, because we were not meant to be the solution to our own problem of sin and brokenness. Guilt in its purest form drives us closer to God. This is hard to believe for many people because guilt can so quickly turn into shame.

Guilt and shame are cousins, but one pushes us to God, and one tells us to run away. Shame is the long-term bad feeling that comes from what we have done or from what has been done to us. The worst part about shame is that it attacks our identity. It will tell us things in our inner being like, "Because you failed, you are now a failure." "You are not worth loving because he left you." "What you have done is unforgivable." Where guilt tells us to run to God, shame tells us that what we have done can never be forgiven, so our only alternative is to run away.

Do you see how slimy shame can be in our lives? It's not just the uncomfortable feeling. That feeling could be a good guilt that God will use to deepen our dependence on him. Shame tells us that we have become the problem. The longer we hold to that false identity, the more damage it is allowed to do in our lives. Eventually, the pain associated with shame becomes overwhelming, and rather than feel it anymore, we become numb. This is the worst side effect of shame. There are far too many people who have become comfortable with the false identity that they adopted from shame. Being numb is dangerous because it makes us stop trying. God has not given up on you. Don't give up on yourself. Only God's grace can heal a heart gone numb. If our shame does not leave us feeling uncomfortable, it can be a sign that God needs to restore our hearts in deep and well-guarded places.

This is why we need radical vulnerability. Vulnerability to God leads to true identity! If we come to God with our feelings of good guilt, he meets us with forgiveness. He promises that he will: "If we confess our sins, he is faithful and just to forgive us our sins and to cleanse us from all unrighteousness" (1 John 1:9). Did you notice that he promises not just to forgive our failures but to cleanse us as well?

When we allow our hearts to be vulnerable to him, he takes away our weak, scratchy fig-leaf cover-ups and meets us with his comfort. In Adam and Eve's case, this wasn't only a promise for spiritual renewal that would eventually come through Jesus but a practical comfort as well. God sacrifices a lamb, crafts them new clothes, and covers them in soft wool. Imagine the relief they felt when they traded fig leaves for lamb's wool! When we resist the urge to cover up, God rewards our vulnerability with comfort, forgiveness, and his righteousness.

NUMBER 3—THEY HEARD

"And they heard the sound of the Lord God walking in the garden in the cool of the day."

Genesis 3:8

As a parent, I know that just saying my kids' full names with my Dad voice gets their attention. It comes in handy if they are about to cross the street without looking both ways. On the rare occasion that I use my Dad voice, I can see a physical reaction of fear wash over their bodies, especially if they are caught in the act of intentional disobedience.

I wish we knew how long Adam and Eve suffered in their fig leaf loincloths. That detail is not given to us. However, I bet it was more than a few minutes because they didn't hear God walking in the garden until the "cool of the day." I believe that God gave Adam and Eve some time to let the implications of their decision wash over them. They had at least enough time to figure out how to sew two sets of the world's most uncomfortable undergarments together and find a hiding place before God came to them in person.

There is a world of difference between "You messed up" and "I messed up." Adam and Eve knew what was coming. They knew that God was going to find them out despite their ever-so-clever undergarment tailoring. Notice how patient God is with them in this process. He saw them disobey the easiest rule ever and believe lies about him. All he had shown Adam and Eve at this point was that he was incredibly kind, generous, gracious, powerful, and life-giving and that he wanted to be with them. God would have been completely within his rights to show up as they were biting the fruit, wagging his finger and proclaiming judgment on Adam, Eve, and all humankind. He did not. He allowed himself to be discovered by Adam and Eve before he even asked them why they were hiding.

Vulnerability would have us come to God even if we are afraid of him. That is easy to write, but when we truly consider the implications of bringing every part of our hearts to him, it can be terrifying. It is easy to *assume* he will react harshly to all the brokenness in our hearts. We struggle to *really* believe that God has the capacity to heal us, forgive us, or love us because we think we are beyond redemption. I know this firsthand because everyone feels like there is a part of them that is beyond redemption. You are not alone. It is in this place that God gives us the gift of time. He gives us opportunity after opportunity to come to him. Call out to him. If we don't, he will eventually call us. If you are really stubborn like me, he might have to use his Dad voice to get your attention. It is worth repeating: There is a world of difference between "You messed up" and "I messed up." It is always better to choose vulnerability rather than be forced to be vulnerable.

NUMBER 4—THEY HID

"And the man and his wife hid themselves from the presence of the LORD God among the trees of the garden."

Genesis 3:8

When you first learned what Jesus did for you on the cross, when you understood that he was dying in your place, giving you unrestricted access to the grace of God Almighty, and adopting you into his family as a son or a daughter, you also received another gift. The gift of the Holy Spirit.

You can't hide. Not if you are a believer. It is absolutely impossible. This might seem strange with as much as you have read in this chapter about trying to hide from God, but it is well-documented by a guy named Jonah: Hiding from God doesn't work. (It didn't go so well for Jonah, or a large fish for that matter, either.) Adam and Eve tried, but they didn't succeed. This truth needs to sink deep into your soul: You, me, Adam, Eve, none of us can hide from God.

I help out occasionally in our church's third to fifth grade boys' Bible study class. The last time I taught the class, I had a student who struggled to control his mouth. By the end of the class, I told him that I was going to have to speak with his parents after class. He was not a big fan of that plan, so he made the mistake of asking me what he had done wrong.

Now, I am not great at remembering details, and I am not a strict teacher. However, I have little patience when people do not respect others in my class. I notice a lot more than my students realize. So I began to list his light misdemeanors one by one, including the ones that I let slide in the moment. By the end of the list, he apologized and changed his attitude for the rest of the evening.

Imagine how even a little bit of vulnerable honesty would have changed the nature of my relationship with this student. If he had come to me at any point and told me that he was struggling, it would have completely changed my strategy for handling his behavior. However, digging in his heels resulted in the opposite of what he wanted. Instead of leniency and another chance, he was reprimanded.

If we continue reading Genesis, we see the same attitude from Adam and Eve. They hide. Then they do everything they can to shift the blame away from themselves. They desperately want to be out of the spotlight at this moment. Resisting exposing our hearts toward God only makes things worse. I want to avoid the discomfort of radical vulnerability as much as anyone else, but I know how destructive it can be to hide from God.

The only way out is through. What is in our hearts will come out through our lives. The hurt we feel from that broken relationship, the pain in our hearts from suffering abuse, the hidden sin we have never admitted aloud, all of the tender places of our hearts are affecting the quality of our lives and relationships. God knows about it all. No matter how much we may want to, we cannot run from his presence. We must receive the life-giving truth that God's presence in our lives is proof that he has not given up on us. He still sees something worth redeeming in our hearts, so he will expose it so that he can restore us.

Vulnerability begins with running toward God. Allow the truth of his presence in your life to transform your reality. Invite him into every place in your heart, especially the broken places. Trust that he will be gracious and merciful to you, and discover the freedom that comes with having no secrets from him.

Father, there is nothing hidden from you. I am amazed at your grace and mercy on my life and that you want all of me, including the broken places. I want to be vulnerable. I want to receive the relational freedom, healing, and restoration of my heart. Holy Spirit, I need you to guide me in this. I need you to show me the places in my heart where I have known there was a problem but ignored it, tried to cover up my shame, heard you but refused to respond, or foolishly tried to hide from you. Forgive me for trying to do it alone. Draw me to deeply trust in you and your goodness. Help me find good people who can handle my vulnerability and point me back to you.

Amen

NOTES

[1] Phil Mason, *Napoleon's Hemorrhoids: And Other Small Events That Changed History*, reissue ed. (Skyhorse, 2019).

[2] Brené Brown, *Rising Strong: The Reckoning. The Rumble. The Revolution.* (Random House, 2015), 4.

CHAPTER NINE

SAFETY IN NUMBERS

One is the loneliest number . . .

The whistle blew, the game began, and my heart pounded in my chest. I had not been this anxious about a live sporting event since I was on the field as an athlete myself. The training regime I had my team on was strenuous. I was confident, as a first-time coach, that my team knew more about the strategy of soccer than any of the other teams in the league that season. We did cone drills, passing drills, ball-handling drills, and even voice commands that I could use to move my players on the field like chess pieces.

The ball was in play, and I was confident that we would not only win but also impress the parents. Two seconds later, chaos ensued. A mass of arms and legs and cleats surrounded the ball like bacteria absorbing a cell under a microscope. Kids were crying and kicking, and the location of the ball seemed to be nothing more than the target for the most intense and enthusiastic to swing their legs. Wide-eyed and with a tinge of panic, my team was engulfed by the amoeba that crawled across the field and, much to my dismay, toward our goal.

We lost that game. I should have known better. Four-year-olds care about one thing in soccer: kicking the ball. (I have never seen so many own goals in my life.) After the game, I assessed the damage and adjusted my team's strategy to account for the fact that everyone on both teams would likely just crowd around the ball and start kicking—regardless of what the coach wanted them to do. In the end, we actually won some games, and more importantly, my kids still play soccer today.

You might be wondering what on earth this has to do with the heart. It has everything to do with the heart. Deep, meaningful relationships begin with a willingness to share our hearts with another person, to welcome someone into our life to be on our team. The only reason that my soccer coaching experience worked even in the slightest was because I got those kids to work together. In the same way, you need to share your heart with others and listen to theirs as well.

In the last chapter, we discussed vulnerability's role in our relationship with God. Just as we found the benefits of deep, uninhibited vulnerability toward God, there are also benefits to being vulnerable in relationships with people. However, when it comes to people, there is more risk involved.

The reason that it is harder to be vulnerable with people than it is to be vulnerable with God is safety. Is God always safe? Absolutely not. Ask any missionary about the risks involved with spreading the gospel to every nation, tongue, and tribe, and you will find a lot of stories of when God's people were put into dangerous circumstances. However, in the Bible, I challenge you to find an example of true humility, vulnerability of heart, and repentance that God does not meet with relational safety and comfort.

If you look back on the last chapter, you will find multiple references to God being gentle, caring, comforting, and many other characteristics associated with safety. While I can promise those attributes in response to your vulnerability in your relationship with God, I would never promise those responses with people. People are far too unpredictable and constantly changing. In fact, there is a very real scenario in your future where you will find the courage to be vulnerable to another person only to have them exploit that vulnerability and hurt you deeply.

I know this leaves us in an awkward position. We hate loneliness. We know we need close community to avoid being lonely, but in order to get that community, we need to be vulnerable with people who will eventually hurt us. That is the risk we take in every human relationship in this life. It is worth it.

If vulnerability with God deepens our connection to him, we can pour gasoline on that fire by deepening our connections with others who are pursuing him. Let me explain: God is an infinite being. By definition, that means he is beyond what any one person could understand. The sliver of his character and identity that any one of us is aware of is handcrafted by him to give us as much of a sense of who he really is as we can handle as an individual believer. Joining with others in pursuit of God gives us access to more of him than we could know about him on our own.

What I know of him is revealed by the same Scripture that you study, but what I know of him is revealed through his Word, my life experiences, my family, my friends, sermons, music, the beauty of creation that I have witnessed, and more. That means that the more you understand my view of God, so long as it is anchored in Scripture, the more you will expand your own view of who he is. Not only this, but we learn so much more through teaching than we do through individual study. What we have learned about God and his nature is to be passed on to others. Without someone to share in our study, we have no reason to formulate a plan for instructing them, and we will miss out on the opportunity to deepen our relationship through teaching. Why else would I be writing this book now? I want to grow in matters of the heart. What better way to become an expert than to go through the rigorous steps of teaching others?

In my story, God has consistently used other people to help me understand my heart. I would go so far as to say that deep relationships with others are the primary way God has revealed my heart's well-hidden areas. While a certain amount of self-discovery happens in my devotional and prayer life, God has used powerful, rich conversations with trusted friends to help me engage with my heart. That is how I learned about the depths of my own heart. It was not easy to find these friends, but they have changed and continue to change my life for the better.

There is a lot to learn about discerning which relationships warrant deeper heart conversations. We want to avoid oversharing our hearts with people who would pull us away from deepening our relationship with Christ. For that reason, let's take a look at what the Bible has to say about loneliness. Loneliness can make us desperate for friendships and more likely to make catastrophic mistakes as we pursue healthy, heart-changing relationships.

CREATED FOR COMMUNITY

"It is not good that the man should be alone;
I will make him a helper fit for him."

Genesis 2:18

In the creation story, God is speaking and singing the world into existence. Light and dark, the sun, moon, stars, plants, animals. And on each one, he put his stamp of approval. He calls them all good. Then comes man, the creation not spoken into being but lovingly handcrafted. Not sung but breathed into life. In the middle of all the goodness of creation, there is one thing that God calls "not good."

To be alone is not good. This is not a sign from heaven to rush off and get married to the first eligible person who stumbles across your path in an attempt to make your life "more good," but rather, I would like for you to take stock of your personal loneliness level. How alone would you rank yourself on a scale of one to ten? Are you pleased with your results? Is there room for improvement?

I would be willing to bet that your heart knows that to be alone is not good because you know the pain of loneliness personally and often. Your physical body is affected by loneliness as well. The National Library of Medicine has done extensive research on the effects of loneliness and has discovered that people with "high levels of loneliness" are at a greater risk of having heart attacks, high blood pressure, and other health conditions. In the overly dense language of the article, "In sum, feelings of loneliness mark increased risk for morbidity and mortality, a phenomenon that arguably reflects the social essence of our species."[1] So there we have it. Loneliness equals not good, just like God said. In fact, it turns out that it is deadly.

Unfortunately, just being aware of the problem is not much help to us as a species. Many studies have shown a sharp increase in feelings of loneliness, especially when the global pandemic forced everyone into isolation for a season in 2020 and 2021. However, loneliness was an increasingly concerning problem long before the pandemic. In an article published by CNBC in January 2020, immediately before the pandemic, Cigna researchers found that "Three out of every five adults, or 61%, report that they sometimes or always feel lonely, according to the second annual Cigna U.S. Loneliness Index, which is based on a survey of 10,000 adults. That's up 7 percentage points from the 54% reading reported from the company's first loneliness survey a year ago."[2]

Let's not move too quickly past the implications of this study. I intentionally found a study done before the pandemic by a well-respected survey company, with a large sample size of ten thousand people, showing that there was a dramatic and sharp increase in feelings of loneliness in the years leading up to the pandemic. It is no coincidence that the first problem mentioned in the creation story, loneliness, started to spike before a pandemic that forced isolation on the vast majority of the people on the planet over the course of two years. We have a real enemy, and he knows that loneliness is a human weakness. The quiet desperation that comes with loneliness makes us act rashly and can even cause us to commit self-harm if not addressed in a healthy manner. Loneliness is not good.

What did Jesus do? Jesus was fully human and felt the whole range of human emotions, including loneliness. He didn't rush into a romantic relationship to alleviate the sting of being alone; in fact, he did not fear healthy forms of isolation. More importantly, he didn't shy away from relationships with others because he was afraid to be hurt. Remarkably, even knowing that he would be betrayed, he still allowed Judas to be a part of every heart-level conversation that he had with the disciples, except for some beautiful conversations he had with them in the upper room and on the Mount of Olives before his betrayal.

Jesus is the perfect example of how we are to pursue healthy relationships within the church. His leadership in this area shows his willingness to associate with anyone, regardless of wealth, status, poverty, gender, race, or outward signs of holiness. He chose a specific number of close friends, disciples, para-disciples, and followers. It is intriguing to see the way science backs up how incredibly genius Jesus was in organizing his relationships with others.

Robin Dunbar is an anthropologist who rose to anthropology fame because of the Internet and the book, *The Tipping Point* by Malcolm Gladwell.[3] In an attempt to research the human mind in relationships in the 1990s, he made a remarkable discovery about human limits. Thanks to the Internet recognizing its significance, *150* became known as "Dunbar's number." The crux of his discovery was that the human brain can only maintain an average of 150 friendships at a given time.

There are a number of different reasons why we can only handle 150 friends, the most shocking being our physical limits. Why can you not have more than 150 friends? Your Instagram and Facebook accounts likely disagree with this hypothesis! It feels like such a small number. For me, that is only a little more than half of the people who attend my church on a Sunday. How am I supposed to be an effective pastor if I can only befriend half of my congregants?

It gets worse; 150 people are not even close friends. Dunbar claims that is the number of acquaintances we can retain at any given moment. The group of close friends does not stem from 150 people. It is contained within that number. Why is it that our brains cannot handle more relationships than 150 people? Let me explain Dunbar's theory this way:

Imagine you are in a conversation with Joe. Your brain is concerned with how you and Joe relate to each other. Mary walks up, and your brain is now concerned with your interactions with Joe and your interactions with Mary. Your brain is now juggling two relationships. That is how we assume friendly group dynamics work, but it is not.

What Dunbar discovered is that your brain subconsciously juggles how you interact with Joe, how you interact with Mary, Joe's interaction with Mary, Mary's interaction with Joe, how you assume Joe feels about interacting with you, how you assume Mary feels about interacting with you, how you assume Joe feels about interacting with you and Mary at the same time, and how you assume Mary feels about interacting with you and Joe at the same time. If you do the math, though only three people are involved at this point, your brain identifies eight very different relational interactions at work.

Imagine how complicated it gets to diagram this out if you add in one more person. What if Bob enters the conversation? What if Bob and Sally walk over to your little group? I hope you can see that 150 relationships in your life represent a very large number of social interactions that your brain is able to juggle.

The other dynamic that limits us to 150 relationships is the problem of time. Every relationship requires some level of time commitment, and as I am sure you are personally aware, the closer your relationship with someone, the more time they require of you. Perhaps a more positive way of saying this would be that the deeper and more beneficial a relationship, the more we must invest time in the relationship. Therefore, being intentional with our relational time management can have a huge effect on the quality of the rest of our life. We only have time to invest in 150 relationships, give or take, so we might as well make the most of them. Any one of them holds the potential to enrich our life, expand our view of God, and help us know our own heart.

Remember that we started at the big number 150, and there are smaller significant numbers contained within Dunbar's number where we will focus most of our attention. Dunbar's research found that there are distinct circles of friendship. I will give the hard numbers, but remember that these are averages of a wide range of people. Dunbar found that in the degree of relational closeness, most people will have groups of friends numbering around 5, 15, 50, and 150 people.

Take a moment and see if these numbers stack up with your experience. Most people will have one to five friends who are as close as family, ten to fifteen or so close friends, around fifty people who would be good friends, and somewhere in the range of 150 people who they would have no problem talking to in the grocery store if they saw them pass by.

The reason I find these numbers fascinating is that they align with Jesus's experience. I believe that the authors of the Gospels spelled out a strategy for building your relationships by showing us Jesus's relationships with his followers. Let's put it to the test and see if Jesus lines up with Dunbar's numbers.

Did Jesus have close-as-family friends? Peter, James, and John were Jesus's closest friends. There are multiple ways to back this up, from Jesus calling Peter a rock on which he would build his church to John calling himself the "one who Jesus loved" and resting his head on Jesus during the Last Supper. My favorite piece of proof that Peter, James, and John were Jesus's best friends was the transfiguration in Matthew 17.

Those three alone were invited to go with Jesus to see him in his glory. In a very real way, they were the only ones who had a chance to know Jesus for who he really is because they were able to see him in a glorified state. Dunbar's tightest relational circle is limited to up to five people, and Jesus chose three.

Did Jesus have close friends? Yes, the next tier of friendship for Jesus was the twelve disciples. This group was nearly as exclusive as the first group. These men knew Jesus intimately. It is safe to say that these twelve had unique access to Jesus's heart and vice versa. It was said that if someone called themself a disciple of a teacher at that time, they would follow that man close enough to eat the dust from his sandals as they followed him. That's close. They shared meals, weathered storms, saw miracles, had honest conversations, and would ultimately die for the sake of this friend (with the exception of Judas, of course). Dunbar's number for the second level of friendship is a range of up to fifteen, and Jesus chose twelve.

Did Jesus have third-tier friends? The third tier of friendship is an interesting one and requires a little bit of biblical detective work. After the resurrection, the disciples decided that they needed to refill the position of the twelfth disciple. Someone needed to take Judas's place. The timing is important. This happens after the resurrection but before the gift of the Holy Spirit arrives in Acts 2. Acts 1:21 and following spell out the qualifications needed to be considered for the job.

> One of the men who have accompanied us during all the time that the Lord Jesus went in and out among us, beginning from the baptism of John until the day when he was taken up from us—one of these men must become with us a witness to his resurrection. (Acts 1:21–22)

Matthias was the name of the man chosen to become one of the Twelve, and this passage makes it clear that he had been quietly in the background anytime Jesus was not sneaking away to pray or inviting only the Twelve into a conversation. He just followed. From Jesus's baptism to after his death and resurrection, Matthias was there. He wasn't the only one.

I believe that Matthias was in a trusted third tier of personal friendship with Jesus. I would even go as far as to give a number to this third tier with an educated guess from Luke 10.

> After this the Lord appointed *seventy-two* others and sent them on ahead of him, two by two, into every town and place where he himself was about to go. And he said to them, "The harvest is plentiful, but the laborers are few. Therefore pray earnestly to the Lord of the harvest to send out laborers into his harvest." (Luke 10:1–2—emphasis mine)

The seventy-two had to be trusted to faithfully proclaim that the kingdom was here. They were given instruction, and they were given trust. Jesus called them laborers in his harvest. Of course, we are not given any hints as to the nature of Jesus's friendship with these seventy-two followers, but I would venture to guess that Jesus knew them all by name, and Matthias was one of them. Not only this, but the trust that Jesus puts in this select group of believers reveals that they knew his heart and his message. They knew the importance of proclaiming that the Messiah and the new kingdom had arrived. Dunbar's third tier of friendship is in the ballpark of fifty people, and I believe that Jesus had seventy-two friends among his followers.

Finally, we will go back to Acts 1 to find out just how many people were there with the disciples when Matthias was chosen, to see the fourth and largest tier of friendship. We know that in Acts 2, explosive church growth occurs, and soon thousands flood to the burgeoning church. But in Acts 1, before the promised Holy Spirit comes, there is a group that devotes itself to prayer. Peter stands and proposes that they should fill Judas's vacant place among the disciples. Acts 1:15 happens to mention that there were 120 people in the room for this discussion.

These people are the ones who believed in Jesus and his resurrection because of the disciples' testimony alone, not because of explosive church growth or a promise of a position in a new movement, or even because of a display of power from the Holy Spirit. They would not have been there if they did not know and believe Jesus. This was before the coming of the Spirit, speaking in tongues, and thousands flocking to the church, while the entire world around them would have called them fools for believing that Jesus, whom they saw crucified with their own eyes, was alive. They had no worldly reason to continue in the way of Jesus, but they did because they simply believed. Dunbar's number for the final tier of friendship was 150, and Jesus had 120.

The important thing to remember is not that science helped Jesus strategize his relationships but that Jesus's strategy for relationships works because humans like us are created to work that way. I believe that some of the people who traveled with Jesus, like Matthias, often felt out of the loop. This has nothing to do with Jesus's inability to love Matthias but everything to do with wise and strategic time management forced by physical limitations.

The same is true of us. Friendships that benefit our hearts take time. No one can jump into a new friendship and pour out their heart in a healthy way without first building trust with the other person. Remember that healthy vulnerability and a feeling of safety go hand in hand.

Some therapists will even go as far as to say that there are only eight basic emotions. All the specifics of our emotional state are built from that limited selection of emotions, all of which are negative in nature except one. That root emotion is the feeling of safety. The theory goes that in order to feel happiness, you must also feel safe. To feel pleasure, you must first feel safe. To feel the warmth of a close and meaningful relationship, you must first feel safe. It is unwise to share your heart with another person without first establishing relational safety.

That is why the one to five people in your inner circle require 50 percent of your relational time. This is confirmed by Dunbar's research. Half of your time has to be dedicated to this group, or they move out to the next tier due to neglect. The amount of vulnerability you have with this group requires trust and is a two-way street. No one person dominates, but all is shared across the friend group. This group is not all serious, not by a long shot. Because it is so safe, it also has the most potential for fun in your life.

The next tier of twelve to fifteen friends will take the next 25 percent of your relational time. If we are using Jesus's example, this group of friends has nearly as much access to you as the people in tier one, and therefore nearly the same level of trust, safety, and fun should exist in this group of friends. This group requires so much time because it is not only participating in life but also processing life together. In my experience, this is the tier of friendship that most people wish they could expand. If you struggle with loneliness, I wager that you struggle to name ten to fifteen friends in this category.

These two tiers together take up 75 percent of the time you have in your life to maintain relationships. To be relationally healthy, we must become adept at relational time management. Not only this, but we must value the limited time we have with people. Most people exist in a constant state of busyness, trying to fill the second tier of friendship by spreading themselves thin on these larger groups of friends. However, if there is no trust built over time with key people, heart-level conversations about life and our relationship with God will not exist.

Once we have established first- and second-tier friendships, it is helpful to remember that they are not stagnant. Every relationship in our life is fluid and moving. The question is, Are they moving with you into a deeper and more meaningful relationship with Jesus? As you draw closer in friendship, do you see more of God?

You may read that last paragraph and think that friendships like that are too good to be true. But those friendships are possible. In fact, they are supposed to be plentiful within the church.

> I appeal to you, brothers, by the name of our Lord Jesus Christ, that all of you agree, and that there be no divisions among you, but that you be united in the same mind and the same judgment. (1 Cor. 1:10)

Unity of mind and unity of purpose require heart-level relationships. My favorite example of this relational design within the church is in John 17. Jesus is praying over the disciples, and then he prays for us. Look closely at the deep level of unifying connection that we are supposed to have with other believers in this passage.

> I do not ask for these only, but also for those who will believe in me through their word, that they may all be one, just as you, Father, are in me, and I in you, that they also may be in us, so that the world may believe that you have sent me. The glory that you have given me I have given to them, that they may be one even as we are one, I in them and you in me, that they may become perfectly one, so that the world may know

> that you sent me and loved them even as you loved me. (John 17:20–23)

That last line gets me every time. "So that the world may know that you sent me." Look closely at that passage again. In this verse, the church is not on the street corner preaching, handing out tracts, giving sermons, or baptizing anyone, and yet evangelism is happening. They are united to such a degree that the world looks over at us and realizes, "This Jesus guy really did come and love these people because they have something I don't have. . . . I wonder if he would love me?"

We, as the church, have really missed out on some of the greatest evangelistic opportunities because we refuse to be united with other believers. And why is that? Because we do not feel safe. We will only reveal our hearts when we feel safe, and we need to take the time necessary to build relationships within the church that start with safety and lead to vulnerability. That is the only way to identify our hearts and to begin to become the unified body that John 17 describes.

Start small. Do not read this chapter, feel left out, and start sharing your deepest and darkest secrets with anyone in the church who will listen. Rather, do the hard work of finding one or two more people. Make sure they are people that you believe you may be able to trust in the next six months. Begin with fun. Begin with safe conversations and build up to deeper topics over an extended period of time.

Take care not to overshare with someone of another gender, especially if you are married or in a committed relationship. This is in no way permission to start or continue an emotional affair. Jesus had only guys in his inner two circles. Mary, Martha, and their brother Lazarus were certainly more than acquaintances, so I would categorize them as third-tier friends. Jesus always treated Mary and Martha as sisters.

Offer your feelings of loneliness to Christ, and tell him all about the pain that it brings. Ask him to bring you friendships that will draw you closer to him. Trust in his timing. Remember that all relationships take time and effort. Continue to pursue meaningful relationships and look for ways that they can help you uncover your own heart.

Jesus, yours is the ultimate example of healthy relationships that I want to follow. I want to know my heart better than I do right now, and I know that trusted people in God-honoring relationships can help me in this goal. Guide my steps and my conversations as I pursue deeper connections with other believers. Bring the right friends into my life. Help me be a blessing to them and encourage them in their relationship with you. Help me know when to speak and when to listen. Give me the patience not to push relational growth on another person, but help me to trust in your timing. Thank you for designing the church to be a place of connection. Please give me the connection that I long to have. May I be a part of evangelizing the world through radical Christ-honoring relationships with my brothers and sisters in Christ.

Amen

NOTES

[1] Louise C. Hawkley and John T. Cacioppo, "Loneliness Matters: A Theoretical and Empirical Review of Consequences and Mechanisms," Annals of Behavioral Medicine 40, no. 2 (Oct. 2010): 218–27, https://doi.org/10.1007/s12160-010-9210-8.

[2] Bertha Coombs, "Loneliness Is on the Rise and Younger Workers and Social Media Users Feel It Most, Cigna Survey Finds," CNBC, January 23, 2020, www.cnbc.com/2020/01/23/loneliness-is-rising-younger-workers-and-social-media-users-feel-it-most.html.

[3] Malcolm Gladwell, *The Tipping Point: How Little Things Can Make a Big Difference* (Back Bay Books, 2002).

CHAPTER TEN

DISCIPLING OTHER HEARTS

It doesn't really matter what I think; Logan thought the ride was terrific. It was billed as "4-D entertainment." The way I see it, 2-D is what you can draw on a piece of paper, a 3-D movie gives you a headache while images seem to poke slightly out from the screen on occasion, and 4-D does all of that while your chair shimmies and a malfunctioning mister blasts you in the face with cold water at intervals.

This all started when my wife and I took our kids for a day of outdoor adventure and excitement at a local attraction. We rode a bunch of kitschy rides, saw some beautiful sights, and were entertained by performers. Now it was time for *Journey 2* (based on Jules Verne's *Journey to the Center of the Earth*). I sat with Logan, my young son, in the theater chairs, seatbelt in place, donning my 3-D glasses and expecting the worst.

While underwhelming to me, Logan thought *Journey 2* was the most engaging and immersive experience of his life. I know that you are thinking, "Just wait until his head is big enough to fit in a decent VR headset," because I thought that too! Ever since we left that theater, he has bragged about the experience to everyone who would listen. Suddenly, that is his favorite movie. It is not just a point of focus for him; it was a transformational experience. It was like being in the movie for him, and now every other movie-viewing experience is going to be compared, not to the reality of what he experienced, but to how he felt while watching that shortened version of the film.

While I know reading a book is not the same as watching a movie, if you have done the hard work of digging deep into your heart, you may find your experience like going to a 4-D movie with Logan. There is something almost addictive about tangibly feeling progress on a heart level. You begin to see your own motivations clearly, and eventually, you can identify them quickly without even having to ask why before finding keys to breakthrough moments. You will see the person you would have become without heart change and thank the Lord that you are on a new and better path. You might even go so far as to bring others into your story, to pursue deeper levels of trusted community to help you become all that God created you to be.

If this resonates with you, I need to issue you a warning. There will be very few people who "get it." They will see the change in your life and ask you what has shifted. They might even pick up this book, but very few will have the guts to apply these lessons to themselves and do the hard work that comes with true heart change. But for you, the more you put the things in this book into practice, the more it will feel like you are seeing things in four dimensions.

After spending my life in pursuit of understanding my heart and its motives, I have discovered that I am constantly discovering motives or hidden agendas on autopilot. I have made such a practice of living with the intentional examination of my motives that I don't have to go through an emotional process in addition to the logical examination of my heart.

This is not to say that I have made it. Or that developing an analytical skill void of emotions is good for me. In fact, I am far from knowing 100 percent of who God created me to be. God continues to issue me a challenge to move past analysis and into a deep relationship with him, emotions and all! It is an adventure I take with him in my heart and its inner motives. This is a joyous part of life! There will always be more to know about who we are because the one who created us is infinitely wise. The complexity of our hearts is one of his most beautiful creations, which we were never meant to see with our physical eyes but our spiritual ones.

It is a gift to discover our own heart. Along the way, we will also begin to know and understand others at a deeper level as well. In fact, with enough practice working through the issues of our hearts, we may find that we know someone better than they know themselves. Most people do not consider their motives, and when those motives are thinly veiled by their words or actions, we begin to see and understand other people's hearts.

WITH GREAT POWER . . .

I made the commitment to refrain from dating in high school. I know it is weird, but for me, it was the right choice. In fact, there was a bit of a movement in the church-going millennial generation that did away with serial dating and decided that courting someone was a better option. This is not a book on dating and relationships in the church. I am not smart enough to write that book, and as far as I am concerned, guiding my own kids through that season of their lives is a future-me problem.

I had many philosophical reasons to back up my decision to not date in high school. I even had some convincing biblical reasons, like Song of Solomon 8:4. The thing is, philosophy or even wisdom from the Bible is motivating to a degree, but there was still a huge part of me that wanted to dive into the dating pool. The thing that ultimately kept me from taking the plunge was knowing my own heart. I could not look honestly at my own heart and find a valid motivation for dating another person that was not completely self-centered.

I wanted a relationship to feel validated as a man. Ultimately, I cared what an immature girl thought about me more than anyone else, God included. Dating with a heart motivation like that would be dangerous. It would give a high school girl power, influence, and responsibility over my heart. Neither I nor the girls I was interested in were ready for that. At the very least, I wanted to approach a relationship with honorable motives. I wanted to get my heart to a place where I would jump at the opportunity to sacrifice my joy and happiness for another person. I knew that my true motives were not pure, so I did not grant myself permission to move forward.

During this time, I also discovered something fascinating. The person who knows other people's deep motives or desires has a lot of power. Honestly, it was concerning and scary. I had to be very careful once I knew more about another person's heart than they knew, to avoid manipulating them. A man who masters even the first few levels of heart motives could use subtlety and persuasion to get any girl he wanted. He could also deliver devastating blows to another person's self-esteem or self-worth. We see hints of this kind of thing being abused. If a girl has a father wound, an "alpha male" can easily control her.

Much like Spider-Man's Uncle Ben, I am telling you now, "With great power comes great responsibility." As an agent of the kingdom of God, you do not have permission or the right to use someone else's heart for your personal gain. Ever. As a bearer of this knowledge, you are now being commissioned to help others find healing. If at any point you find yourself stepping on someone's heart to try to climb in your career or get that key relationship, you must stop and start over with your heart.

In fact, now that we are equipped with the wisdom that comes with knowing our own hearts, if we sense that something is out of place in another person's heart, there is a good chance that we have a responsibility to help. We are not required to help everyone. In fact, people who feel that they have to help everyone are often overwhelmed, stressed, and driven by their guilt. This is not at all the freedom in Christ that we are discovering through his presence in our hearts.

We should actively pray for discernment from God to help us figure out where he has called and equipped us to help others discover their hearts. In my life, God has always answered my prayers that start with me saying, "I want to serve you and your kingdom, not my agenda. Please help me discover what that is." At every stage of our lives—high school, college, career, newly married, parenthood, and beyond—there are areas where we have influence through our relationships. Those areas of influence shift over time, and the amount of impact we can have on others shifts as well. Here are some general guidelines that we can use to help us grow in discernment, regardless of the season of our lives.

People who are not in the kingdom of God can benefit from examining their outer-level issues, but they will never see the life-changing effects of true heart change without Jesus. If we are helping someone with their heart and they refuse or are not ready to deal with the core issue of unbelief, they will not experience a full breakthrough. While simply living an intentional life and questioning our motives is a powerful skill to develop in life, remember what we learned in the early chapters of this book. The role of the Holy Spirit in matters of the heart cannot be overlooked or downplayed. We and the people we want to help all need the Spirit's intervention and guidance.

Knowing what is going on in someone else's heart does not mean we are the person to intervene. As a high school boy who was obsessed with understanding how the heart operates, it did not take long for me to figure out that high school girls would be attracted to a guy who even attempted to understand them. It was not my job to be their counselor or confidant. I had to work hard to set up limits, and even then, I ran the risk of leading girls on. If I felt that it was God's calling on my life to be the solution to these girls' insecurity, it would have ruined their lives and mine as well.

Some people are simply not ready. Just because we are passionate about discovering our hearts, that does not mean everyone is ready to go on that journey. We are setting ourselves apart by pursuing our hearts. Most people want to be part of the crowd. In fact, they want that so much that they are willing to believe the thinnest and most ridiculous lies they tell themselves rather than face their true selves. If we try to force them into vulnerability, we will find that they protect those lies and insecurities with fists, teeth, and a vicious tongue. It is not our job to change anyone's heart. It is Jesus's job.

On the rare occasion that you do have a responsibility and a right to speak into another person's heart, don't expect drastic results. Patience is the key to drastic heart change. I wish I could have a dramatic encounter with Jesus and that he would work some crazy miracles in my life, showing me exactly what to do next and how to operate my heart, but that is not how he has worked in me. There has not been a satisfying and instantly gratifying turning point in my life that was not preceded by at least a year of hard work and persistent prayer. I want things deeply, but God does not usually give them to me quickly. God is wise, and I benefit more from him leading me in this slow manner. I believe that if you look back over your life, you will find the same thing to be true for you. It would be inconsistent, then, to assume that simply because God chooses to use us in someone else's life, they will experience dramatic change over the short term. Remember, my mentor Tab allowed me to struggle for a whole year before I discovered that I was stubbornly refusing to believe simple truths about God in the center of my heart. We are called to have the same kind of patience as we guide others to their hearts.

We will rarely be asked. I was the first person in my church's history that asked to be an intern in the worship ministry. I have asked only a handful of people in my life to mentor me, and more than half of them were so shocked by the request that nothing ever happened. If you need a mentor and don't have one, that may be because you have not asked for one. On the other hand, someone who needs you may not have the courage to ask. Do not fold your hands over your lap after reading this book, sit back, take a deep breath, and expect that someone who needs the key that you now hold will waltz into the room and ask for your help. Prove yourself by studying Scripture, continuing to work on your own heart, being vulnerable with your own struggles and wins, and helping others incrementally. The few who approach you after you have proved yourself in this way will truly be ready to discover their hearts.

DISSATISFACTION AND SUPERFICIAL RELATIONSHIPS

One of the most challenging seasons of my life was entering the career field after graduating from college. My wife and I moved away from our home state of Tennessee to go to LA (Lower Alabama). Our experience in college was unique. There were roughly one thousand students at Bryan College at the time, so there were plenty of opportunities to know everyone casually. Pair this with some of the richest relationships of my life, and it is no surprise that a rich community was a natural byproduct of my time in school. I did not know what I had at the time.

I remember talking to graduates and being warned that their real-world experience after leaving college was a rude awakening, but nothing prepared me for the loneliness that we felt after we left school. In the years that followed, we always lived close to some school friends while in Alabama, and that was a huge lifeline. However, all of us felt the pang of loss that comes from longing for a community that includes dozens of close friends.

At first I thought it was just me and Emily who felt like we were living in a relational vacuum. Years later, I started talking to as many of my alumni friends as possible, trying to discover if any of them were able to find a satisfying community experience postcollege. Every single person, married or not, still in the college town or not, felt like they lost their community after college and have struggled to rebuild that sense of relational closeness.

This is not right. I challenge you to read through John 17:20 and following to prove that it is not right. We have a lot of work to do in the church to build a community that can rival that of a small college campus. However, that is another book for another time. What I can tell you is that the first step toward fixing the problem is allowing ourselves to be dissatisfied.

I know that we as Christians are supposed to value contentment in all circumstances, and yes, there is a sense in which that is true. During persecution and imprisonment, Paul wrote Philippians 4:1–13, which tells us we can endure all the hardships of life that come with both persecution and success through Christ who gives us the strength. However, there is also a sense we get in Scripture that there is no limit to the benefits of knowing God.

During Jeremiah's life, the Scriptures were lost. When they found the scrolls again, Jeremiah said, "When I discovered your words, I devoured them. They are my joy and my heart's delight, for I bear your name, O LORD God of Heaven's Armies" (Jer. 15:16 NLT). These are not the words of a man who is chill and content. Jeremiah would not have set up his Bible angled just the right way with his half-caf mocha cappuccino partially in frame while a blueberry candle burned so he could get the perfect shot for his Instagram post. No one devours something if they are satisfied. No one discovers anything if they are content.

The beautiful tension we are called to live in as Christ's followers is one of contentment of circumstance but never contentment of relationship. This is why matters of the heart are so important. We may find that examining our hearts with the help of the Holy Spirit does change our circumstances for the better a little bit, but it will drastically affect the way we relate to other people. I, for one, have seen a multiple-decades-long process of God creating compassion for others in my heart. It used to be much easier for me to drop truth bombs and leave people to pick up the pieces on their own. Now God doesn't let me do that anymore. I have grown in my compassion, and I genuinely want to help others by guiding them toward the truth and allowing them to discover it for themselves.

If you resonate with the sentiment that the church needs to provide you and others with better relationships, then don't be satisfied with the relationships you have. This is not permission to complain but permission to take action. There is a false stereotype in the South that men are unable to be vulnerable or real about their lives without a fishing pole in their hands. The general idea is that to build friendships with other guys, you have to play golf, hunt, fish, kayak, or do a project with your hands. While all these things are good and can be tools to help some people open up, this approach as a church's only strategy to build a brotherhood of men is not working.

I pick on men's ministry because women's ministries tend to dive into issues of the heart more easily, but there is still more that they can do to help foster a community where openness, vulnerability, and heart transformation can occur. From my wife's experience, things at a women's conference may go well, but in the weekly grind, it is easy to feel disconnected from other women in the church.

The point is that this is not a call for new versions of men's or women's ministry, but that we cannot depend on the "extra stuff" like events to produce real and lasting results in the church. Statistically speaking, there is no event that will transform the world, a minuscule chance one could impact your community, and only a slightly larger chance that one event would help your church over the long term. What can make an impact on your church, your community, and ultimately the world is radically different relationships between believers.

However, those relationships cannot exist if the people involved are not committed to growing in Christ. Growth in Christ looks like emotional, spiritual, and mental health all rising in tandem. This is what heart transformation looks like. If you are able to find people in your church who are willing to grow like that, your church is well on its way to making a huge impact on the world for the gospel.

AUTHORITY

I have a love/hate relationship with authority. I love it when I feel like I have it, and I hate it when I don't. Something in the way I am wired makes me feel more at peace when I am in the driver's seat. Even when it comes to coaching my kid's soccer teams. There have only been two seasons that I attempted to be a parent and not a parent-coach. I deeply regretted that decision both times. As a dad, I am a spiritual authority for my family. I am confident in my ability to coach elementary-age children to play soccer, but the stakes are a lot higher when I consider the responsibility that comes with being a spiritual authority to my wife and children. I don't think I am ever supposed to feel like I am fully capable of fulfilling that responsibility. In fact, I feel poorly equipped in my own strength to lead my family. Leading them has been one of the most intense ways that God has shown me I need the Holy Spirit

If you are not at a point in your life where you are a spiritual authority to another person, someday God will likely call you to be an authority. There are no motivational pep talks that can turn you into someone who can handle a role like that overnight. God does the work of maturing and shaping you over years. Don't rush him. Take the time to do the work on yourself so that when the time comes, you are well-equipped with the tools you will need to lead others. Notice that I did not say to work so that you will be ready. I have never felt "ready"; I have only felt a greater sense of my need for God.

Move slowly when you do have spiritual authority in someone's life. Pushing people too hard can not only make them prickle up, but it can have other disastrous effects as well. In my upbringing, humility was often platformed as a desirable trait. Of course, I wanted to be honored for my humility, so I pursued being humble. This is hard to do when you are being trained to be a worship leader. People tend to tell you that you did a good job if you do a good job. This made me uncomfortable because I was trying to remain humble.

The advice I received from my mentors was to redirect compliments to my team. "I am blessed to have great people to work with" became my standard answer. Something still felt weird about the whole process, but at least I felt like I was being humble. The problem was that I always felt like the person giving the compliment was frustrated that it didn't stick.

Years later, I attended a songwriting conference led by some of my spiritual heroes at the time. It was a small conference, so I was able to corner the keynote speaker and thank him for all that I learned through his podcast and online resources. He looked me in the eye and said, "Thank you, I receive that." He did it in a humble manner, but it made me, as the one offering the kind words, feel like what I said was truly meaningful. As the one offering the compliment, it felt good to have it stick. Still, I wanted to be humble, and receiving the praise didn't seem like the right application.

Years later (again), I was obsessed with figuring out how to best respond both outwardly and in my heart to compliments after leading worship. That is when I discovered Bob Sorge's book, *Dealing with the Rejection and Praise of Man*. As you can imagine, the lion's share of the book is centered on making sure that your identity is wrapped up in who you are in Christ, not in the praise or rejection of people. Right near the end of the book, my question was finally answered.

I will sum up Sorge's lesson like this: There are two steps to take when someone praises us. The first is to acknowledge in our hearts that all the praise belongs to God alone. I am not in the business of trying to steal his glory, so I redirect the honor to where it belongs, with God. The second step is to recognize that when someone is offering us a compliment, they are courageously attempting to communicate that God has used us to do something good in their heart. We can look them in the eye and simply say, "Thank you." They are offering themselves to us as a friend. They want us to know that they understand us better and feel a relational, good, and biblical connection to us. They will not have the words to express this connection, but they may have the courage to tell us "Good job."

I wanted to go through this lesson I learned in detail to show you that as someone in authority, even if you are well-intentioned, if you are putting your own spin on what God is trying to work in another person, it can take decades to unravel. In some cases, people get fed up with the inconsistency of advice and choose to walk away from Jesus rather than side with opposing mentors. This role is not to be taken lightly, and most people will have authority at some point in their lives.

In a worst-case scenario, sending those under our spiritual authority on the wrong path in their hearts can lead them to depression, low self-esteem, and feeling judged. It can feel like walking a tightrope to make sure that what we say and how we say it is consistent. It is possible to have authority over another person's heart, especially a child, and communicate loving correction and freedom from the bondage of sin. It is also possible to communicate judgment, disappointment, and anger because of unmet and unrealistic expectations.

There is a way to help those under our care to feel empowered to do the hard work of discovering their hearts. Affirmation, unconditional love, grace, and regular reminders that we want what is best for them are powerful tools if we are in a position to disciple the heart of another person.

God, I need wisdom, guidance, and discernment. I understand that the discovery of my own heart comes with a cost. I understand the responsibility that I have to become a trustworthy person. Please help me grow in purity and in dependence on you. May I never think that I have all the answers, but may I be quick to find you in prayer, even with the matters of the heart that seem easy. Holy Spirit, guide my words and motives toward other people, and may I be an agent of community growth in the church.

Amen

CHAPTER ELEVEN

LEARNING TO LISTEN

"I just don't know what to do. I mean, I know what I want to do, but I also want to make my parents happy," my friend confided in me, struggling with what to do after college. I replied, "No, you don't; you are not even scared that your parents will be mad. You are just afraid to disappoint them." She rolled her eyes at me, told me I was right, and that she sometimes hated how well I knew her. The crazy thing is, I didn't know her that well. I was listening. It wasn't what she said, but an unmistakable tell that betrayed her fear of disappointing her parents that flashed across her countenance as she talked about them. My job at that moment became clear: to show her what she was hiding from herself—that her parents were still controlling her decisions.

Listening to others can be an incredibly powerful tool in the life of the believer. So much of life is enhanced by our ability to listen or deteriorated by our unwillingness to listen. When it comes to the heart, being able and willing to listen is a skill we cannot ignore. Those who are serious about winning in their own hearts are constantly asking God about what he is doing in and through them. Not only this, but if we care about others' hearts, we must learn to listen if we want permission to help them.

"Out of the abundance of the heart the mouth speaks" (Matt. 12:34). The heart fountain works constantly. Not only are we to pay attention to what is coming out of our own hearts but also out of the hearts of others. This is the foundation on which a true biblical community is built, so it is worthwhile to invest in the skills needed to be a beneficial part of that community. Not only this, but some of the greatest joys in this life come through deep, intimate relationships with others. Learning to listen to the heart enriches conversation, deepens trust, and is an incredibly loving act.

Developing our listening skills is also a great way to benefit our lives as a whole. Any good negotiator knows the importance of listening well and communicating in a way that shows the other person they have heard and understood their side, even if they do not agree. Success in marriage depends not on being a good listener but on the commitment to grow in our ability to listen to our spouse. Understanding another person more intimately than any other on the planet takes time and commitment. It also does not happen without intentionality.

One of the areas I am intentionally working on right now in my listening journey is with my son. When my son Wyatt was nine years old, he had one of the most vivid imaginations. He still does! I don't say that just because he is my kid, but because it is true. I have worked with plenty of kids that age in ministry, and the way that his brain works is like none other. For example, he is into animals and Pokémon right now. He will create an entire world in his head and fill it with creatures that he has invented himself. He will design his own Pokémon cards, complete with attack points, weaknesses, and element types. He knows each one, all of their evolutions, and every detail about each character. He is incredibly creative and impressive to watch.

However, Wyatt expects me to be able to listen to his descriptions of this make-believe world and retain all the details about the characters as flawlessly as he is able to recall them. Being much more of a visual learner, I struggle to keep up with him. However, I try not to shut him down when I get lost in the imaginary world because, to him, it matters. If I can listen to Wyatt now, there is a much better chance that he will let me listen to him later when he has life-altering questions. In fact, I have already begun to see the benefit of giving him my valuable attention. We have had rich conversations about how to handle difficult friendships, draw courage from the Lord even when we are scared, and understand eternal matters.

The most important part of listening is safety. If you get nothing else out of this chapter, retain this: No one feels heard if they do not feel safe. Safety can be built in fun, like imaginary world-building, co-op video games, a cup of coffee, or a fishing trip, but ultimately, people are trying to discover if we will listen and whether we will use that information to help them or harm them.

That is why we must talk about how to listen to God before we discuss techniques for listening to others. Listening to God is a skill that, much like listening to people, takes time and intentionality to master. While I cannot promise that you will hear an audible voice from the Lord, I can give you some tools and best practices that will help clarify his voice from the myriad of other voices rattling around in your brain.

The first and primary way to listen to God is through Scripture. God has given us the Bible, which we unironically call "God's Word." We call it that because, though it was written down by men, it was inspired by the Holy Spirit. God has provided in his Word everything we need to face every situation that this life will throw our way. That is not a promise that he will make anything easy, but that he is speaking to every situation.

Scripture also has all the information we need to access our hearts and to live a full life surrendered to God's will. If he created us and gave us life, then it makes sense that his Word would give us a game plan for making the most of that life. The beginning of our journey to being able to identify God's voice is to familiarize ourselves with that voice by knowing the Bible.

Being familiar with Scripture is like setting up a filter in our hearts for God's Word. What if we are at work and we suspect that the office bully is bad-mouthing us to our boss? Is there a part of the Bible we can reference to figure out what to do? How about Daniel? The king was tricked into punishing Daniel for praying to God (which he was doing five times a day, BTW). God used this opportunity to shut the mouths of lions that had likely been starved for days to ensure that they would tear apart anyone who was thrown into their den, making Daniel a representative of God's glory to the king.

An example from the New Testament is found in Philippians.

> Do not be anxious about anything, but in everything by prayer and supplication with thanksgiving let your requests be made known to God. And the peace of God, which surpasses all understanding, will guard your hearts and your minds in Christ Jesus.
> (Phil. 4:6–7)

We know just how valuable it is to have our hearts guarded. Do you feel like your heart and your mind are guarded by Jesus himself? How much confidence would you gain in your life if you were to put this verse into practice? The way we access this Christ-guarded heart is by placing every anxiety and request that is in us at the foot of the cross. Only then does the peace of God guard our hearts and minds. This means that any voice we are listening to that encourages our anxiety is not from God. That is a powerful truth to carry into our day! If what I think God may be saying to me causes me to feel at peace and aligns with the rest of Scripture, it is probably God speaking.

There are a number of other ways that God speaks to us. I think one way that many people try to hear from God is through podcasts. Either listening to sermons or a Christian-run podcast that discusses life with strong believers is a wonderful way to hear from the Lord. However, it should not be the primary way that we connect with Jesus. What God has called us as individuals to create, become, accomplish, disciple, train, or evangelize in this life is not the same thing for everyone else. He created each of us as an individual to do things only we can do to advance his kingdom. So we can't rely solely on another person's spiritual revelation to carry us to where God has called us.

In the same way, close relationships can be fuel to the fire of our relationship with God. They can help us decipher what God is saying to us and help equip us with all we need to accomplish his will in our lives, but they cannot do the work for us. We are not supposed to go through life alone. We are also not supposed to be copycats of another person's calling. One of my closest friends, who was also a worship leader, recently stepped down from his ministry position to pursue songwriting. The similarities between his calling and my own are many, but God has not called me to do the same thing. I had to listen and pray a lot to come to this realization.

We have focused a lot on how we listen to God's voice, but there are two more tools that we must engage before we are able to listen to him with confidence. They are prayer and the Holy Spirit. Prayer goes hand in hand with listening to God. He loves to hear from us and to know our hearts intimately. Would you like it if a friend or sibling gave you the silent treatment for months, only to then ask you for favors? If we want a deeper relational connection with those we call close friends, God wants that as well. Prayer is a primary connection point in our relationship with God. Have we shared our hearts with him through prayer lately? We should not assume we will be able to listen to him without being willing to talk to him.

This brings up another common issue within the church. Do we really want to hear what God has to say to us? I have met many people who struggle to hear from God because if they are honest with themselves, they don't really want to listen to him. This can stem from a number of factors. If we have experienced childhood trauma, resolved or unresolved, it can be difficult moving forward in our relationship with God to trust that he is good. If we don't believe God is good, then we will likely fear what he will say to us.

Another common reason in the church that people are apprehensive to hear from God is because of their relationship with the Holy Spirit. In many Christian contexts in the United States, the Holy Spirit is the most overlooked part of the Godhead. In fact, that is an understatement. Many Christians are flat-out afraid of the Holy Spirit. The arguments surrounding what constitutes a work of the Spirit in our modern context have caused many believers to avoid him altogether.

Making Christians willingly disconnect from communion with the Spirit is one of the most devastating attacks from our enemies in the kingdom of darkness. Think about it: Jesus himself said, "Nevertheless, I tell you the truth: it is to your advantage that I go away, for if I do not go away, the Helper will not come to you. But if I go, I will send him to you" (John 16:7). If I were trying to harm Jesus's plans, I would come up with a strategy that creates a rift between the Holy Spirit and believers.

Take stock of your own heart. Is there any part of you that is resistant to the Holy Spirit? When was the last time you prayed to the Holy Spirit? Do you love this member of the Godhead? If you do find resistance in your heart, stop reading and talk to him. Confess that you have avoided him, and tell him that you want his intimate involvement in your life. The more you are able to make yourself aware of his presence, the more you will find that you are able to hear him speaking to you.

I spent two summers going through an internship at my church that was focused on worship leadership. There were a number of responsibilities that came with the position, including, but not limited to, janitorial duties, a three-hour-long prayer meeting every Thursday, and a required reading list provided by my mentor, Fred. My expectations for the reading list were that I would be reading books on leading worship, leadership skills, and music theory. I eventually got to those books, but in my first year through the mentorship, every book I was assigned was about one topic: Listening to God.

The first book was *The Practice of the Presence of God with Spiritual Maxims* by Brother Lawrence, who was a monk in France three hundred years ago. His responsibilities at the monastery were not glamorous but limited to work in the kitchen. The book itself is less of a book and more of a compilation of letters written to those who recognized Brother Lawrence's intimate and constant awareness of the presence of God. He advised those who wanted this same communion with God to be in constant prayer in the midst of their menial tasks as well as in the important moments of their days.

Other books assigned to me that summer were *How to Listen to God* by Charles Stanley, *Hearing God* by Peter Lord, and *The Pursuit of God* by A. W. Tozer. Since I was a young guy, you would think that Fred was giving me the tools I needed to make big decisions in my life, like where to attend college, how to choose a spouse, or what career to pursue. However, our conversations about listening to God centered on this concept of communing with God at all times, including during worship services. Overwhelmingly, the message of these books was that the best way to hear the voice of God is through the familiarity that can only come through time spent with him.

In my case, that meant that if I wanted to be able to identify what the Holy Spirit was communicating to me while I was onstage leading worship for my church, I would only be able to trust that voice if I had spent ample time with him during the week. The same is true with your life. If you want to hear the Holy Spirit, spend time with the Holy Spirit. Don't worry if it is awkward at first or if it feels like you are having a one-sided conversation with him. All time spent in an awareness of the presence of God is time well spent.

Another tool that I learned through those books was the value of silence. There is a big difference between a long silence on a first date and driving in silence with our best friend. The silence on a first date feels awkward because there is a lot riding on each moment spent with the person across the table. The comfortable silence between friends is not awkward because we know each other. There are no unmet expectations because we accept each other for who we are. The same can be true in our relationship with the Holy Spirit.

A major reason why we struggle to hear the Holy Spirit may be because we spend all our time with him doing the talking! In my life, the regular practice of shutting my mouth and making space to listen to God was when I was able to identify his voice with clarity. Now, for me, God's voice is not audible but comes to me as thoughts that did not originate in myself. It is important to me to clarify this because there is a lot of vague talk surrounding God's voice. I can't speak to the validity of any other person's experience with his voice, but I am happy to give you the details about my experience listening to him.

Here are some tips for making space for God to speak to you. The books referenced above have many more, but I will point out the ones that work in my life.

DON'T BRING AN AGENDA

It is easy to ask God a specific question about what is most important to us and then expect that he will give us a direct answer to our question. I would encourage you to look at the Gospels and see how rarely Jesus responds to questions directly. Most of the time, he would tell a story, ask another question, or teach a lesson. That doesn't mean that he will never give us direct answers, but it certainly isn't his normal strategy. Oh, and by the way, what he chooses to speak to us is always better than what we want him to say, so we can pray that he will help us remove our agenda when we make space for him to speak.

REMOVE DISTRACTIONS

If we need to post it on Instagram, it doesn't count. Don't worry about aesthetics or having your Bible turned to a particular page. Don't burn incense or a candle, and don't play any music.

The ultimate goal, strange as it may seem, is not actually to "hear" from God but simply to sacrifice our time and be available for him. At the beginning of your time, I would encourage you to pray something like: "God, I am here with all my problems, concerns, and agendas. I want to lay them aside and trust that what is important to you is more important than what concerns me. I am listening, and I would love to hear your voice. I am available for you . . ." Notice that there is no "Amen." This is intentional. You don't want prayer to end. You can remain in prayer without saying anything to God. Just make time for him and listen.

It is also important to note there is no excuse that excludes us from this practice. We are in control of our schedules, and we make time for what is important to us. I can't think of anything that supersedes a deeper communion with God. Susanna Wesley, the mother of John and Charles Wesley and their eight siblings, knew the value of time spent with God. If anyone gets a pass for not having daily time with the Lord, it would be Susanna. However, she would daily take a chair, place it in the middle of the kitchen, sit down with her Bible, and pull her long apron up over her head. The kids knew not to bother her during this time and also were to take her example and spend time in private devotion while the apron was up. How important is time with God to you?

STATE OF MIND

The temptation is to think that what I am encouraging us to do is meditation. While there are many similarities between the two practices, there are some key differences. Meditation is a practice that has its roots in transcendentalism. That is a big word that encompasses many world religions like Buddhism, Taoism, and Unitarianism. The basic shared beliefs are centered on the idea that the spiritual realm is more real than the physical and that the ultimate goal is to become one with everything and, therefore, part of God. Christianity borders this philosophy because we believe that there is a very real spiritual world. However, Scripture is clear that the physical world is not an illusion but a present reality. Also, believers have the Holy Spirit indwelling them, but this is different from believing that we as humans are part of God. We are made in his image, but in no way are we equal to him.

I make this distinction to clarify that while meditation can be a valuable Christian practice, I would caution those practicing it to distance themselves from the Eastern mysticism that is taught with this practice. Some of the key transcendental ideas that are pushed through meditation are an emptying of the mind and a welcoming of all spiritual voices. We do not want all voices speaking to us, just one specific voice. In fact, I often say out loud that the enemy is not welcome during this time in the name of Jesus. Don't be fooled into thinking that this pursuit of God will go without spiritual attack. So in your quiet, intentional practice of listening, make an effort to quiet the voice in your mind, but ask the Lord to help you identify his voice alone. As a practice to quiet my mind, I will often read the Psalms until the worries or concerns of my day begin to fade. Then I close my Bible, ask the Lord to speak, and listen.

⁂

These practices are just that, practices. There are many times I do not feel like I hear from God, and that is okay. Remember that the point is to be available. There is one thing I can promise you: He is speaking, and when you hear him, it will involve your heart. The most common experience I have when listening to God is hearing from him about a dark corner of my heart that I have yet to explore with him. The depth of the relationship that happens between God and me when he guides me to discover his design in my life is astounding. He so wants to be involved in your development and spiritual growth. Don't depend on sermons and podcasts to endlessly fascinate you with things about him; do the work to know him, and it will transform your heart.

One of the unexpected ways I have heard God's voice is through the mouths of trusted friends as well. Not only am I able to hear God's voice, but he may also want to speak through me to others. This is an incredible thought if we ponder it for a moment. God does not just want us to isolate ourselves with him endlessly, but he wants us involved in his mission, his plan, and sometimes as his messengers to the people we love most in this world. Now that we have spent a lot of time picking apart the ways we can hear God's voice for our own benefit, it is only right to look at the ways God speaks to others through us.

If we want to be able to speak to someone's heart, we must first be able to listen to people. Yes, developing listening skills is yet again the key to accessing the heart, only this time, it is someone else's heart. Communication is a complex human skill. It is worth some effort to become better at communicating with others because that is the foundation on which our relationships are built. We will find that as we grow as listeners, we will grow in our ability to affect heart-level change in the lives of the people around us.

When it comes to learning to listen, not just hear, I love the example that the ancient Chinese give us. The ancient Chinese symbol "ting" means "to listen." At first glance, it just looks like a complicated series of strokes on the page, but it is packed full of meaning. In fact, it is made up of six separate symbols that teach us to listen on a heart level.

As this image portrays, the symbol is made up of six individual symbols. The symbol for you, ear, eyes, undivided attention, heart, and king are all found in the word. I was taught this particular lesson by my friend Wimberly Sims, who passed away recently. She embodied these six characteristics so well and used them daily to build meaningful relationships and to speak truth into the lives of those close to her. Let us examine each part of this word.

You: The listener holds responsibility in the conversation. They are to feel the responsibility to create space for the conversation to happen and to be present and active. Inasmuch as a conversation involves one person speaking, it involves another person receiving, processing, and valuing the information that is communicated. This means that the listener has just as much responsibility to be present and active in listening in order for even the most basic forms of communication to take place. It is all about being present and available for another person.

Ear: This makes sense because we need physical hardware in order to hear. This reminds me of the old saying, "You have two ears and one mouth so that you can listen twice as much as you speak." The trick is to listen to what is actually being said. So often we are tempted to use selective hearing to absorb only what we want to hear, or worse, to listen for points of disagreement. If you want to know another person's heart, you must be willing to hear what they actually say. True listening takes in the full content and context of the conversation as it is without opinion. This means that if any content or context is lacking, it is the listener's responsibility to ask clarifying questions to make sure they understand both. An additional way to double-check that we are using our ears is to repeat what we think we heard so that we know if we understood correctly.

Undivided Attention: This is a discipline of good listeners that can only be developed through intentional practice. It was certainly easier in ancient China when people were not bombarded with four thousand to ten thousand ads per day like we are, according to a study referenced by *Forbes*.[1] Distraction is a part of life. It is not a healthy part of life, but a part nonetheless. We can work to push past our short attention spans. This shows that we genuinely care about the person who is speaking. It communicates value in the relationship and protects the listener from the pitfalls of selective hearing. It also ensures that we are not thinking of what to say next while someone else is speaking. Discipline and practice are the only ways to develop undivided attention, but it is a vital skill for anyone who wants to become a good listener. This is also the most outward-facing way to communicate to another person that we are concerned about their heart.

Heart: This directly connects to our purposes in this chapter. A good listener is empathetic. They really care. They are able to connect emotionally with the speaker and, in doing so, communicate back to them that they are not alone. Empathy is the key to unlocking the places where the speaker feels isolated or stuck. Listening with the heart moves beyond logic and even beyond the spoken words and seeks to understand the emotional component of the conversation. Strong beliefs and emotions are often linked to past experiences, and a listener who is compassionate can find understanding even without agreeing. Developing your heart to be a listening heart is how people feel that you not only care but understand who they are.

King: This is the symbol that I found most surprising. It seems to sum up all the other characteristics of a good listener well. The idea is to listen to others as if they were the most important person in the world. I have never met a president or a king, so it is hard to know for certain how I would act. I do know that I would be respectful, listen intently, and measure my words carefully. Do we truly value the person we are talking to like God values them? If we ask God to help us feel how he feels about someone, we will automatically begin to care more.

As we develop as listeners, it is important to remember that the goal is not to spout our own wisdom but to simply be available to encourage others to become more dependent on God as the source of true wisdom. One of the best ways to do this is to ask questions. When we find ourselves at a loss in a conversation, we can simply repeat back to the person what we think we heard, see if there are other perspectives that need examination, and never be afraid to say, "I don't know." There is no shame in failing to have the advice someone is seeking. Our goal is to understand their heart and help them discover it as well.

Questions are more powerful than answers. In my small group, my mentor Tab kept pressing in, trying to help me figure out my own motives. Why, why, why did I keep going back to the same sin patterns? What was pushing me there? Selfishness? Yes, so why would I choose selfishness? Anger? Yes, so why would I run to the comforting burn of anger? This went on for a number of weeks until I was finally able to land on the root of the problem in my heart. I was struggling to believe that God could provide for me. Tab didn't tell me that, and I am so glad he did not spoon-feed me the answer. I had to go down the path of why myself. The difference between asking God to help me with my selfishness versus asking God to forgive my unbelief is night and day! The relief and the weight lifted from me were astounding! I understood my heart, and it was all because God used Tab's listening ear and good questions to keep me motivated to go deeper into my heart. My prayer is that you would do the same for someone else.

Father, Son, and Holy Spirit, I am coming to you now without an agenda. I am laying aside my schedule and my anxiety, and I am not even going to ask you for anything right now. I am just here and available for you. I am listening if you want to speak to me.

NOTE

[1] Jon Simpson, "Finding Brand Success in the Digital World," *Forbes*, updated April 14, 2022, https://www.forbes.com/sites/forbesagencycouncil/2017/08/25/finding-brand-success-in-the-digital-world/.

CHAPTER 12

CONCLUSION

In the early 2000s when I was in high school, there was a huge push in youth groups for purity. In fact, it was such a strong push that many millennials now look back on that time and the strategies that the church used with a bad taste in their mouths. I am sympathetic to this reaction. Some of the key figures from that movement have not remained faithful to the call of Christ into adulthood. A lot of the events were also very pushy in their messaging.

I remember one event in particular that was put on by a nationwide abstinence program called "Silver Ring Thing." The goal of this program was to target unchurched students through abstinence messages. This ministry has since shifted focus and messaging and is equipping students to live a life for Christ with new strategies, but I remember attending an event. It was a huge venue with all the bells and whistles that come when a youth leader has access to an unlimited production budget. The lighting changes and smoke effects were nonstop, the onstage games were high energy, and to say the speaker was passionate would be an understatement.

At the end of the event, if we were committed to being abstinent until marriage, we could purchase a sterling silver ring for seven dollars. Now, I want to be clear: I love a good light show and smoke machines. I love a good flashy show and passionate speaking. In fact, more often than not, that is what I prefer to do myself when given the opportunity to speak in front of a crowd. However, even I came away from the event feeling like there was a lot of show put in front of me to get me to sign a card, hand over a few bucks, and wear a ring. There was so much pressure focused on getting me to make a commitment that it made me feel like there would also be a lot of support as I did the difficult part of fulfilling that commitment.

Now, women were not exactly throwing themselves at my feet, but the simple reality of knowing that I would be waiting not just one or two but multiple years before I was married was daunting. Where are the light shows and rock bands for the people who fulfill the commitment? Where is the passionate message for the college student, freshly dumped, crying in the dorm alone? I think that my generation has struggled with purity culture in the church because the focus was on making a commitment, not on equipping us to fulfill the commitments that we made to God.

It is tempting for me, as the author, to take this last chapter as an opportunity to double down on the commitment that you need to make to dig deep into your heart. I know from experience that getting you to make a promise is not enough. I did attend the Silver Ring Thing, and I did pay seven dollars for a ring. I was regularly asked in high school if I was married, because I wore the ring on my left hand ring finger. I was picky when it came to the people I would date. I courted my wife, and we waited until marriage. In fact, my wife and I had our purity rings melted down and cast into a single ring that is now my wedding band. However, in the grand scheme of things, the event did nothing but give me access to cheap silver.

Yes, I did fulfill my commitment, but not because of any contract I signed. Understanding the benefits of sex exclusively in the context of marriage did not help me keep my commitment either. Even having access to a healthy accountability group, while that was a huge benefit, did not help me keep my commitment. The only thing that helped me keep my commitment and ultimately set up my marriage for success was the consistent examination of my heart and its motives.

The only way I fulfilled my commitment was by being honest with my own heart. I invited a few trusted friends who were committed to the same things that I wanted in life, and we loved each other in accountability. I certainly did not do everything perfectly (I even have anxiety over figuring out dating and relationship guidelines for my children), but I did not do it alone, and I did not do it without intention.

I have attempted to give you the same thing in this book. A gift of central truths about the heart that you can use over the long term to see breakthrough and change in your life. You can use the examination of your actions, the acknowledgment of your motives, and the affirmation of your belief in who God is to live out your true and powerful purpose on this planet. Ironically, if you do this regularly, you will find that it will grow a particular Christlike attribute in your heart and life.

PURITY

Yes, that word that is loaded with so much baggage in my mind is actually one of the most beautiful gifts that God has to offer us. It is a word that should feel unattainable yet desirable. If you are like me, you may feel a slight pang of guilt, but ultimately, this is what Jesus is offering us. Remember that at the end of all things, purity becomes our clothing. When you and I are given our fully redeemed and new bodies, we are clothed in white, clothed in purity. Remember that this is not something we earn but something Jesus is offering. He will help us access it through our hearts.

"God blesses those whose hearts are pure, for they will see God" (Matt. 5:8 NLT). This verse smacks me right in the face. Think about it. There is no bad news at all in this verse. Take the first two words, "God blesses." Who doesn't want to be blessed? Even better, it is a blessing from God! In fact, here in the South, the word *blessed* has lost a lot of its original meaning. We say things like, "Bless your heart" (which is the most devastating insult you can give to another person while somehow still appearing to be nice), "Bless my soul," and "Bless you" after someone sneezes.

The true meaning of this word is less like a fairy waving a magic wand, someone giving you a thumbs up, or even finding money lining the walls of your house. If you have ever seen *Thor: Ragnarök,* there is a part where Thor is getting ready to participate in a gladiator-style fight against his will. His opponent crashes through the doors and into the arena in a spray of rubble to reveal the Hulk. Thor takes one look at him and smiles wide, saying, "YES!" That "YES!" sums up the word *blessing* very well.

Imagine walking into a room and your best friend has no idea that you are going to be there. They look at you, eyes wide, smile wider, and say, "YES!" I know you want friendships like that. Can you wrap your head around the truth that God wants a friendship like that with you as well? He wants to look at your heart, see it as pure as Jesus's smile, and shout, "YES!" That response from God is far more valuable than the blessing of money, fame, notoriety, comfort, or power.

The crazy thing is, not only is he willing to bless us, but he is even willing to do what needs to be done in our hearts so that he is able to bless us. That's what the next portion of the verse is about. It is well established that the more we hyperfixate on our bad habits, the more we are likely to continue them. For example, if you want to lose weight, don't eat cookie cake every day at lunch. Don't even think about cookie cake. I don't care if it has the chocolate buttercream frosting on it; push cookie cake out of your mind. Cookie cake is only appropriate for eating at children's birthday parties. The only acceptable version of cookie cake is chocolate chip, and you certainly shouldn't eat any right now. You shouldn't even envision a cookie cake in your mind at any point while reading this book . . .

Now that you have wiped the crumbs from the corners of your lips and picked the book up again, you can see why the approach of the Silver Ring Thing failed. It doesn't matter how true or well-intentioned the message is or if it's delivered with appropriate passion; if the message is a list of rules or dos and don'ts, it will not be effective. That is the whole point of the Old Testament. God kept giving the people rules to show them how impossible it was to meet his standards. In response to their own failures, the people added more rules rather than admit that they needed God to intervene.

Don't be like that. Purity of heart is a lot more about admitting we need God to intervene and remind us of our true identity in him than it is about covering up messes. Purity is more than covering up or atoning for sexual sin. Purity of heart is the courage to be truthful and vulnerable with our hearts to God and to another person. In the uncovering of the hidden things, God begins to work his healing. Be brave enough to bring them into the light and see how God will do the work of making you pure. That is what the middle of this verse is all about.

"God blesses those whose hearts are pure, *for they will see God*" (Matt. 5:8 NLT—emphasis mine). My favorite part of this verse is the last bit. I wanted to first make sure that we understood the context of everything leading up to this point. I want to make it extra clear that God blesses and that God makes our hearts pure so that we can now learn what it means to see God. This does not make logical sense, and that is why I love it.

If you are like me, you have a tendency to keep a scorecard in your relationship with God. Like, "I have done my devotions today, called my grandmother, and helped someone load their groceries into the back of their car. Therefore, God is allowed to bless me." Or maybe you feel like God is punishing you for your sin. Either way, that is not how this verse, or the truth of Scripture, works in real life. First of all, Romans 8:1 tells us that God doesn't punish us for our sins if we are in Christ. He may discipline us to train us, but there is no punishment because of our wrongdoing. In the same way, God is not obligated to bless us in the way we want him to just because we obey him. He is God, and he gets to do what he wants!

Matthew 5:8, however, gives us a huge clue as to what God's plans are for us. He wants us to know him. Is there more to this life than to know the one who gave it to us? He wants to be the fulfillment of the deepest desires of our hearts. That is why it is worth it to pursue knowing who we are. The more we know ourselves, the more we are willing to be honest with ourselves, the more he purifies our hearts, and we discover much more than who we are. We discover who God is.

The beautiful thing about this whole process is that we are not the ones behind the steering wheel of our hearts, guiding ourselves to where God longs to reveal himself to us. God himself is in charge of this adventure. If you are reading this now, God is at work in your heart to show you something about himself. Don't let this moment slip by without acknowledging that God is at work. Take him seriously, and lean into this promise from Matthew 5:8. He will bless you because you are pursuing a pure heart, and God himself is the truest fulfillment of that promised blessing.

Along the way, the byproduct of discovering your heart will be a greater awareness of yourself. You will discover all the wonderful things that God has created you to do in your unique way. You will find your calling in life. You will know deeply how your inner being operates and how to find work to do that is fulfilling. You will know the mechanics of why you do what you do, and ultimately, you will be able to change any unhealthy behavior or attitude by using the truth you find in Scripture to combat the lies that you believe.

You will also notice that you know more about what is going on in another person's heart than they know of themselves. You will be equipped to lead them, to guide them to greater awareness of themselves. You will help them find the same fulfillment that you sought when you first picked up this book.

All of this is wonderful, but all of this is simply water flowing from the fountain of a healthy heart. This heart knows the immense benefits offered to it through the truth of Scripture, but it also knows that the greatest gift God has given us is himself. Go deep into your heart. Go with others who can lead you, and go with others who need your leadership, but as you go, find Jesus. He is the gift to discover over and over again in the heart of the believer.

WISDOM

We have already looked at Proverbs 4:23, the verse about guarding your heart because it is a spring of life. In fact, you could say that this whole book has been about that verse and how to put it into practice. However, a lot is said before this iconic verse that gives us a glimpse into the heart of the passage as a whole.

> The beginning of wisdom is this: Get wisdom,
> and whatever you get, get insight.
> Prize her highly, and she will exalt you;
> she will honor you if you embrace her.
> She will place on your head a graceful garland;
> she will bestow on you a beautiful crown.
> (Prov. 4:7–9)

If there is one attribute of God's character that we need to focus on developing in our own lives in order to get better at navigating our hearts, it is wisdom. In fact, Proverbs is centrally focused on wisdom. God offered Solomon one request, and he chose wisdom, and God liked that answer. Therefore, the practice of understanding your heart and how you interact with it is a wise practice.

I love the way the ESV translates verse 7. If you feel like you want to apply what you have learned in this book but have not yet been able to bring yourself to start, this verse has the answer. Verse 7 is saying that if we want wisdom but don't know where to start, we can't assume we are standing anywhere but the starting line. One of the most dangerous mindsets we can adopt is assuming we know more than we know. Even worse, believing that we are more experienced than we are. Experience is the best teacher, and until we go down the path of actually discovering more of our hearts with Jesus's guidance, we will not be able to understand ourselves and we will not be able to understand other people.

There is a humility that we must be willing to put on like a jacket when it comes to matters of the heart and matters of wisdom. Arrogant people make terrible students. To get started, we have to admit that we don't know what we don't know. This is not just a practical statement, but God himself will not allow us to make progress without humility. He makes that clear in James 4:6 when he says that he will be in opposition to the prideful. However, he will be gracious to the humble. Knowing ourselves is an act of grace. It is a gift that God wants to give us. Pursue true humility before him and allow him to start the process.

The second way that verse 7 applies to the lessons in this book is that it tells us to take action. There is a big difference between wisdom and knowledge. British journalist Miles Kington is credited with this quote that has made its way into a meme: "Knowledge is knowing that a tomato is a fruit; wisdom is knowing not to put it in a fruit salad." Both wisdom and knowledge are valuable in their own right, but one can transform us from the inside out. Unfortunately, just reading a book does not automatically give you possession of all the benefits of an unlocked heart.

Think about it this way: I have often had to read the manuals of complicated electronics. Sometimes this is helpful, like when I discovered a better way to set up some of the equipment that our church uses to power the sound system. However, in that instance there was one manual involved, and all I was looking for was what would happen when I turned a key. This is helpful, but if all I did was to look at the manuals of each element of our church tech—from the computers to the soundboard to the cameras, the lighting system, the projection system, the lights themselves, and more—at a certain point, I would have theories and opinions about the best way to make it all work, but I would be totally unequipped actually to run any of the technology on a Sunday morning. No one would trust me to do that, nor should they.

In the same way, this proverb is telling us that if we see the value in pursuing our hearts with Jesus, that will not be enough. Having the knowledge of what we should do is not enough. We have to make the decision, right here, right now, to be brave enough to take action. We must choose to be vulnerable before God and other people. We might have to pick up the phone and call or text a pastor, spouse, or trusted friend. We have to ask for help, and we have to start with action. It will be uncomfortable at first, but it is worth it to see God at work in our lives in a new and fresh way.

Don't settle for letting your life slowly float by. Don't settle for comfort when you are offered an adventure with Jesus. Take up your cross, take up the responsibilities of caring for your soul, and see how rich and deep the well of God's goodness and grace is for you. You were made to be a formidable force for good in the kingdom of God, and life is too short for you to waste your time second-guessing if God is willing to use you for a greater purpose.

HIGH PLACES

I want to remind you one last time about Jeremiah. If you remember from the early chapters of this book, he was the one who helped define the bad news about our hearts. Primarily, we looked at this verse: "The human heart is the most deceitful of all things, and desperately wicked. Who really knows how bad it is?" (Jer. 17:9 NLT). Jeremiah's message was not an easy one to receive, and that same tone of "bad news" is prevalent in his prophecies. While there are glimpses of hope, and much like Ezekiel he looks forward to the heart of stone crumbling, overall, Jeremiah's message is one that is desperate for people to turn to God.

The most fascinating thing about Jeremiah's life and message is the time period during which he lived and prophesied. He was a prophet, delivering messages of repentance during the reign of one of the most dedicated and faithful kings the nation had seen since David. Josiah was only eight years old when he became king. At sixteen, he began to research what David believed. At eighteen, he began the process of destroying all the idols and pagan forms of worship that had infected the nation of Israel. Second Chronicles 34 goes into detail about how he went about cleansing the nation. It took six years. Then he began restoring the temple of the Lord. All of this happened without a Bible. When the Law (at the time, this is what they called the first five books of the Bible) was found, Josiah tore his clothes, longed to repent, and apologized for how his ancestors had turned from God.

Next, Josiah gathered the entire nation of Israel to the temple and read aloud all five of the books that make up the Law. He then publicly renewed the covenant with God and promised to follow God's commands before the people. This is how chapter 34 ends: "So Josiah removed all detestable idols from the entire land of Israel and required everyone to worship the Lord their God. And throughout the rest of his lifetime, they did not turn away from the Lord, the God of their ancestors" (2 Chron. 34:33 NLT). This is a slam dunk compared to most of the other kings in Israel's history!

If we are reading Scripture, one of the best tools we can use is looking for repetition. Anytime something is repeated, it is important. This also means that if something is repeated often and then it is not repeated, it is supposed to stand out. There is a small detail in Josiah's story that sticks out like this. Josiah is in rarefied air as being one of the few kings that God affirms by saying that they did right in his sight. However, Josiah and his great-grandfather, Hezekiah, are the only two kings that got rid of the "high places."

During the reign of other good kings, they never completely purged the land of pagan worship. Scripture will say things like, "Jotham did what was pleasing in the LORD's sight. He did everything his father, Uzziah, had done. But he did not destroy the pagan shrines, and the people still offered sacrifices and burned incense there. He rebuilt the upper gate of the Temple of the LORD" (2 Kings 15:34–35 NLT). As we read through Kings and Chronicles, if we look for the high places to be destroyed, we get excited when Hezekiah and Josiah finally are able to take them out! They didn't cave to peer pressure and allow the people, even in a few out-of-the-way places, to continue to practice evil. Yet once their reigns ended, the pagan worship flooded back.

Jeremiah is a strange prophet from the outside because he seems overly brutal in his message to a people who, by all outward appearances, are doing the things God is telling them to do. However, knowing what happens after Josiah dies, we can see that Jeremiah's message was appropriate. Josiah may have removed the high places of pagan worship, and the people may have even said that they would turn back to God, but their hearts were never changed. We must do whatever we can to avoid this happening to us. We must be willing to actively engage our hearts. We must know what they are doing and continue to push them closer to Jesus.

What we do does not matter as much as what is in our hearts. That is an easy truth to say, but how are we daily in the process of directing our hearts' desires toward God? It is possible for him to change the things we long for, the things we value. There are things he may put in our hearts that are better than what we can imagine. He has plans and purposes that we are a part of accomplishing while we are here on the earth.

Life is short; it is a vapor. Take every opportunity to get out of it all you can. That is not a challenge to put a lavish vacation on a credit card, but a challenge to get to know your creator. He wants to reveal himself to you, and he will do that primarily through Scripture. He will also show himself to you through trusted relationships and as he purifies your heart. Don't miss out on all he has for you. Take him up on his word and draw near to him. Trust him, and you will find him to be trustworthy. Let him show you your heart.

God, I am not going to be satisfied with reading a book or going through the motions. I want whatever you have for me to discover in my heart. Help me to do the hard work required to unlock the barriers that keep me distant from you. Give me strength and help me see the long-term benefits of a life spent dedicated to knowing who I am because of who you are and what you have done for me. Fill me with your strength and grace, and lead me now as I learn who you have created me to be.

Amen